D0913062

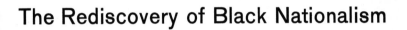

The Rediscovery of Black Nationalism

Also by Theodore Draper

The Six Weeks' War

The 84th Infantry Division in the Battle of Germany

The Roots of American Communism

American Communism and Soviet Russia

Castro's Revolution: Myths and Realities

Castroism: Theory and Practice

Abuse of Power

Israel and World Politics

The Rediscovery o

NEW YORK / THE VIKING PRESS

Black Nationalism

THEODORE DRAPER

First published in 1970 in a hardbound
and Viking Compass edition
by The Viking Press, Inc.
625 Madison Avenue, New York, N.Y. 10022

Published simultaneously in Canada by
The Macmillan Company of Canada Limited

SBN 670–59114–9 (hardbound)
670–00295–x (Compass edition)

Library of Congress catalog card number: 70–104163

Printed in U.S.A. by The Colonial Press Inc.

Second printing February 1971

To Sidney and Frances Alexander
affectionately

Foreword

I first became interested in the subject of black nationalism in the 1950s, when I was working on the first two volumes of a history of American Communism. In the second volume, *American Communism and Soviet Russia,* I included a chapter on the origins of the policy then known as "the right of self-determination of the Negroes in the Black Belt." This policy was conceived in Moscow and came as a surprise to most American Communists, even those in leading positions. As I worked along, I wondered whether there had been any native American antecedents for this or any other kind of Negro nationalism. I found that the phenomenon had an ancestry going back at least a century but that the American Communists had not known of it at the time and had not made use of such precedents until much later. In the end, however, I could refer to the matter only briefly, and I put away most of my notes for almost a decade.

As the demand for Black Studies arose in the past two or three years, it occurred to me that the current manifestations of black nationalism might be better understood if its history were better known. I took out my old notes and went over the ground again, and the result was a lengthy article published in *Commentary* magazine in September 1969. For this book, however, I tackled the subject for the third time. Though I have kept the general framework and some passages of the article, the present work is more than twice as long and has given me the opportunity to rethink, re-examine, and revise many of its sections.

My chief aim has been to relate the past and present of black nationalism. Much remains to be done in this field, as the absence of a single serious study of even "the father of black nationalism," Dr. Martin R. Delany, indicates. I have tried to tell his story at some length, for the first time, but he obviously deserves a full-scale biography. Moreover, I have tried to deal with only one aspect of the historic American Negro problem; it raises further questions which go far beyond this self-imposed limitation, some of which I touch on in the concluding chapter—with no illusions about how much more needs to be done in both theory and practice. It seemed worth while to do as much as was feasible for me to do within the confines of the subject and my own capacities to deal with it. I also wrote this book in the belief that the problem is at least as much white as black and that it must be faced by both whites and blacks for their mutual salvation.

Finally, I am indebted to the Hoover Institution on War, Revolution, and Peace, at Stanford University, and to its Director, Dr. W. Glenn Campbell, as well as to the Institute for Advanced Study, at Princeton, N.J., and to its Director, Dr. Carl Kaysen, for enabling me to work freely and independently.

Contents

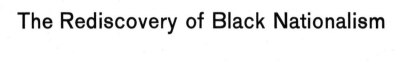

The Rediscovery of Black Nationalism

Colonization

1

The resurgence of "black nationalism" was undoubtedly one of the main currents of American history in the 1960s, and it may become even more important in the 1970s. This resurgence has manifested itself in Black Studies or Afro-American programs and departments in our universities; in the Black Panther, Republic of New Africa, and other militant movements; and in the vogue for Afro styles in dress and hairdos. What is not so clear is the meaning of these manifestations. Why has black nationalism taken these forms? Where are they heading? What is the relationship of black nationalism to the past experience of other ethnic groups, such as the Irish, Italian, and Jewish? To what extent is it related to other nationalist revolutions in the so-called Third World, such as the Algerian, with which the black nationalists like to identify themselves?

An awareness of the deeper roots of black nationalism may help both blacks and whites to understand and to cope with the peculiar nature of the phenomenon today. For black nationalism in the United States is not new. Its antecedents go back in American history for well over a hundred years. This does not mean that the problems of yesterday and today are altogether alike. Black nationalism today is similar to and yet different from its manifestations in the past; it is related to and yet distinct from all other nationalisms in the world today. This mixture of the old and the new, of similitudes and incongruities, is what makes contemporary American black nationalism so confusing and frustrating to black and white alike. The confusion, if not the frustration, may be lessened by setting the present-day phenomenon in a larger historical perspective, for which it is necessary to know something of its past. And whites as well as blacks have contributed decisively to this past.

Traditionally, black nationalism in the United States has taken two predominant forms. The first was "migrationism" or "emigrationism," and it is still with us today—if only in fantasy. Paradoxically, this idea was as much white as black in origin. That this was deeply embedded in the white consciousness, two of the greatest and loftiest Americans, Thomas Jefferson and Abraham Lincoln, may serve as witnesses. The ambivalence with which they treated the Negro problem of their day has its counterpart in our time.

Jefferson had no sympathy for the institution of slavery. The words "all men are created equal" were his. He tried to persuade his fellow Virginians that slavery was a "great political and moral evil" and that a large, growing Negro population, whether slave or free, was a "blot in this country." Yet Jefferson and others of his generation were torn between the recognition that slavery was an indefensible human enormity and the conviction that black and white human beings were not made to live together in the same country. In his

Notes on the State of Virginia (1781–82), he expressed the suspicion that "the blacks, whether originally a distinct race, or made distinct by time and circumstances, are inferior to the whites in the endowments both of body and mind." He proposed a plan to the Virginia Assembly for freeing all slaves after they had reached the age of maturity. But, once freed, the plan called for them to leave the country and settle elsewhere. This was the germ of the idea of colonizing the emancipated slaves in a faraway place. In the same *Notes,* he invoked God's wrath against the "unhappy influence" of slavery: "Indeed I tremble for my country when I reflect that God is just; that his justice cannot sleep forever; that considering numbers, nature and natural means only, a revolution of the wheel of fortune, an exchange of situation is among possible events; that it may become probable by supernatural interference!" Toward the end of his life, in his *Autobiography* (1821), he summed up his belief: "Nothing is more certainly written in the book of fate, than that these people [Negro slaves] are to be free; nor is it less certain that the two races, equally free, cannot live in the same government." Despite his convictions, Jefferson freed only a few of his over a hundred slaves because he felt that his financial obligations took precedence.

Jefferson's views were typical of early anti-slavery opinion. In 1790, for example, Ferdinando Fairfax, another eminent Virginian, took up Jefferson's idea and worked it out more concretely. He suggested that Congress should acquire a colony in Africa and provide for the transportation of free blacks who would eventually earn their independence.[1] * Such plans, based on Africa, the West Indies, or the then "Western lands," were common at the turn of the century. They showed that anti-slavery sentiment was one thing, living with freed slaves another.

A half-century later, the same dilemma haunted Lincoln. He loathed the institution of slavery as "a gross outrage on

* Reference Notes begin on page 185.

the law of nature." Yet, as he revealed in a speech at Peoria, Illinois, on October 16, 1854, slavery was one thing, freed slaves another. After denouncing the "monstrous injustice of slavery," he admitted: "If all earthly power were given me, I should not know what to do, as to the existing institution. My first impulse would be to free all the slaves, and send them to Liberia,—to their own native land." But to do so, he immediately recognized, presented insuperable practical problems. Yet he hesitated to free them and hold them here as "underlings." He went on uncertainly: "What next? Free them, and make them politically and socially, our equals? My own feelings will not admit of this; and if mine would, we well know that those of the great mass of white people will not." Without much enthusiasm, Lincoln came out for "gradual emancipation" as a possible course.

In a speech at Springfield, Illinois, on June 26, 1857, Lincoln worried about the prospect of racial "amalgamation." The only way to prevent it, he said, was by arranging for "the separation of the races." To achieve separation, he fell back on Jefferson's old recipe, colonization. As late as August 1862, over a year after the Civil War had broken out, he told a delegation of free Negroes in the White House that the two races were incompatible. "It is better for us both, therefore, to be separated." Lincoln arranged this meeting to induce American Negroes to emigrate, preferably to Central America. When his views were publicized, as he had intended, Negro protest meetings were held to condemn them.[2] And only about four months later Lincoln signed the Emancipation Proclamation, which more than anything else doomed emigration projects, including his own, by giving Negroes more hope in America than ever before—and perhaps ever after. Yet as late as April 1865, just before his death, Lincoln wrote to General Benjamin F. Butler: "But what shall we do with the Negroes after they are free? I can hardly believe that the South and North can live in peace unless we get rid of the Negroes." He still advised: "I believe that it would be better to export them all to some fertile country with a good climate, which they could have to themselves." [3] The most acute judgment of Lincoln's position was probably made by Frederick Douglass, the outstanding Negro abolitionist: "Viewed from the genuine abolition ground, Mr. Lincoln seemed tardy, cold, dull, and indifferent; but measuring him by the sentiment of his country, a sentiment he was bound as a statesman to consult, he was swift, zealous, radical, and determined." [4]

From Jefferson to Lincoln, "colonization" was the white man's favorite solution for the Negro problem. It was no mere case of wishful thinking; it was the basis of the first important Back-to-Africa movement. That it was conceived and organized by whites did not make it less so. In fact, it helps us to understand as much about the white as about the black background of the problem.

The first important Back-to-Africa movement was called the American Society for Colonizing the Free People of Color in the United States. It was founded in the chamber of the House of Representatives in Washington, D.C., in December 1816. The president of the American Colonization Society, as it was also called, was Justice Bushrod Washington, a nephew of the first President. Among its backers were James Madison, James Monroe, Andrew Jackson, Daniel Webster, Henry Clay, and many other distinguished figures of the period. Its chief support came from what would be called today the "white power structure."

The scheme itself was the brain-child of a Presbyterian clergyman, the Reverend Robert Finley of Basking Ridge, New Jersey. It was reserved for free Negroes only, of whom there were about a quarter of a million by 1820. Finley's motives were "benevolent"—he was appalled by the misery and ignorance of the free Negroes in the North, including those in his own parish. He believed that they were capable of improving their condition, but not in the United States.

God, he said, had intended them for Africa, and to Africa they must return—with the help of whites who did not know what to do with them. To Finley, Negroes were always "Africans." He conceived of arranging for their mass migration back to Africa with government support. The country would get a good return on its investment by establishing an African colony on the model of Sierra Leone, the British colony that had been settled in the late eighteenth century by liberated slaves. The whole scheme, which Finley was sure came from God, was calculated to appeal to the greatest number and the most varied motives: the free Negroes themselves; missionaries; empire-builders; trading interests; Southern whites who wanted to get rid of those Negroes whom they feared the most without touching their vested interest in slavery; well-meaning Northern whites who saw it as a form of "emancipation" that might ultimately offer a way of buying out the slave system without recourse to force.

A tremendous amount of propaganda and organization went into this effort. In 1819 Congress appropriated $100,000 to establish a government agency in Africa, ostensibly to resettle victims of the slave trade. The first shipload of would-be colonists arrived off the coast of Sierra Leone the following year and were promptly struck down by a mysterious plague. But the Colonization Society persevered and sent a naval officer whose grandfather had signed the Declaration of Independence to the African coast to buy land. In December 1821 he succeeded in purchasing Cape Mesurado, three miles wide and thirty-six miles long, for less than $300, though not without placing a pistol at the head of the native king. This tiny area was named "Liberia" (after the Latin *liber*, for freeman), and its first settlement was called "Monrovia," in honor of President Monroe. But it was an anomaly—the colony of a private organization, not a United States possession. After many ups and downs the Society decided to get out of the colonization business, and that is how the free Republic of Liberia, by then grown to 43,000 square miles, was born in 1847. The former colonists, who numbered at this time no more than 3000, became its black ruling class, which held down and exploited the native population—even in the form of outright slavery, the ultimate irony—with as much determination as white imperialists elsewhere. The Colonization Society itself started to go downhill in the late 1830s and was virtually finished off by the Civil War.* Its most recent historian, Professor Philip J. Staudenraus, summed up its end: "With it perished dreams of an African empire, an all-white America, and a gradual and peaceful obliteration of slavery." [5]

In effect, the pre-Civil War white Establishment wished to foist African nationality on the American Negro. It did so for the same reason—the incompatibility of blacks and whites—that later Negroes wished to divest themselves of American nationality. Even enlightened whites widely believed before the Civil War that freedom was not a solution to the Negro problem, and that is one reason why it did not become a solution after the Civil War. The roots of the problem went back as much to the Negro freemen in the North as to the Negro slaves in the South. Most white Southerners did not want Negroes as freemen, and most white Northerners did not want freemen as Negroes.

What is more striking about the Colonization Society's effort was the Negro freemen's reaction to it. If they had wanted to renounce American nationality in favor of an African nationality, the Society was made to order for them. The Society's propagandists and agents labored prodigiously to convince the freemen that it was in their best interest to leave the United States, where they could never hope to obtain dignity and equality. The overwhelming fact is that, in

* After a long period of dormacy, the Society was formally dissolved in 1964. But it was reorganized in the spring of 1969 with an all-white Board of Directors and a segregated all-black board of "Afro advisers," evidently in response to and in order to encourage the new separatist wave among American Negroes (*New York Post,* October 6, 1969).

the heyday of slavery, the Negro freemen overwhelmingly rejected the Society's blandishments.[6] There were some, such as Lott Cary, ordained a Baptist missionary and appointed the Society's agent in Africa, who said: "I wish to go to a country where I shall be estimated by my merits, not by my complexion; and I feel bound to labor for my suffering race." But, to do so, he had to become the paid agent of a white society, and—to add to the symbolism of his role—he came to a sad end in a gunpowder explosion, preparing to attack or defend himself and his associates against a hostile African tribe. Two other well-known converts of colonization were the Reverend Daniel Coker of the African Methodist Episcopal Church, and John B. Russwurm, the first Negro college graduate (from Bowdoin College, Maine, in 1826) and co-editor of the first Negro periodical, *Freedom's Journal,* published in New York City in 1827–29. This pioneer Negro organ was zealously opposed to African colonizationism, and when Russwurm changed his mind in favor of colonizationism, he was forced to resign.[7]

But Cary, Coker, and Russwurm were not typical colonists. The vast majority went to Liberia less for political or ideological reasons than to improve their material existence or to obtain their freedom. For every one of these three, there were thousands on the other side who considered them at best misguided and at worst almost traitorous to the best interests of the American Negroes, especially the slaves. The sentiment of the vast majority of free Negroes was most movingly expressed at a mass meeting in New York City in 1831: "We are content to abide where we are. We do not believe that things will always continue the same. The time must come when the Declaration of Independence will be felt in the heart, as well as uttered from the mouth, and when the rights of all shall be properly acknowledged and appreciated. God hasten that time. This is our home, and this is our country. Beneath its sod lie the bones of our

fathers; for it, some of them fought, bled, and died. Here
we were born, and here we will die." [8]

From a very early date, then, the rejection by most
Negroes of an incipient black nationalism was based on
trust in white America's own political and ethical code,
represented by the Declaration of Independence and Christianity. If the Founding Fathers and the Christian churches
had fully lived up to that trust, there would have been no
raison d'être for black nationalism in America. By accepting
in principle that "all men are created equal" but excepting
the Negroes in practice, and by setting aside "Negro pews"
in Christian churches, the Fathers and the churches did
more for black nationalism than the black nationalists were
able to do for themselves.[9] The wonder is not that there
were any black nationalist tendencies but that they were so
few and weak.

The figures speak more eloquently than anything else. In
1852 there were about 435,000 free "persons of color" in the
United States. By that year the Colonization Society had succeeded in sending only 7836 to Africa, of whom almost half
went in return for manumission. In fifty years, at a cost of
$2,500,000, the Society transported only 12,000.

Another form of early colonization was also white in origin.
By 1860, on the eve of the Civil War, about one-ninth, or
500,000, of the total of approximately 4,500,000 Negroes in the
United States were free. Most of them had been manumitted
by their owners. Some of these white owners were not satisfied merely to free their slaves; they bought land and tried to
settle them in their own communities. From these early efforts, which invariably proved disappointing, a more ambitious movement of organized Negro communities arose.
White philanthropists and reformers sponsored the first ones,
then Negroes themselves took over the idea. The best known
of the early white-sponsored colonies was established at Nashoba, in west Tennessee, by Frances Wright, the famous

British reformer. She conceived of a plan to purchase Negro slaves and to train them for freedom. Jefferson and other notables praised her enthusiastically. But, like Jefferson, Miss Wright believed that an inevitable "barrier" separated blacks and whites, making their coexistence impossible. Thus she undertook to train slaves not to live in the United States but for colonization elsewhere. Her plan was really a variant of the American Colonization Society's scheme. The Nashoba colony existed for only about four years, 1826–30, when she admitted failure and sent her slaves off to Haiti. Other Negro-organized communities in the United States and Canada were more carefully planned, but the results were, as the historians of these idealistic ventures put it, "tragically inconsequential." [10] The lesson seemed to be even then that the American Negro problem could not be solved artificially or synthetically outside the United States, hard as it might be there.

It may well be, therefore, that the most fateful decision was made in the early nineteenth century, if not earlier, by the Negroes themselves. The die was cast when the ancestors of today's free Negroes refused not only to go to Africa but to countenance pro-African propaganda. For better or worse, they decided that there was more hope in America, despite slavery in the South and discrimination in the North, than in any other place offered to them. Where we are put down on earth—to what nation we belong—is generally not a personal decision, and fate plays no small part in choosing our nationalism for us. The great mass of American Negroes preferred to wage an uphill battle to become part of the nationalism where they were born rather than to take the risk of losing what they had without gaining what they were promised. There was in this folk decision an irreducible human element of simple attachment to a birthplace that could not be swayed by intellectual persuasion or political manipulation. It should not be hard for later generations to understand why some black Americans went to extreme lengths to escape white oppression and persecution. But it also should not be so hard to understand why far more black Americans, from the same depths of resentment and indignation, refused to take or even to approve of these escape routes.

A century and a half ago, then, the issue of Negro nationality arose. Was it American or African? Influential whites insisted that it was African; Negroes, with relatively few exceptions, insisted that it was American. In the end, through a tortuous combination of circumstances and the most mixed of motives, the Negroes prevailed. Of all the ironies in this story, none is more haunting than that a peculiar form of black nationalism was first encouraged by whites. The "Back-to-Africa" movement was in its inception mainly a white man's fantasy for Negroes.

Emigration

2

The overwhelming majority of American Negroes rejected the white man's fantasy. Yet a black version of essentially the same fantasy also appeared.

As early as January 4, 1787, eighty Boston Negroes petitioned the state legislature to provide sufficient funds to pay for their passage to and to buy land in Africa. They wanted to leave America, they explained, because their circumstances were "very disagreeable and disadvantageous." In return, they hoped to spread the Christian religion, improve international relations, and promote U.S.–West African commerce.[1] The Massachusetts legislature was apparently unmoved by the plea.

In that same year, the Free African Society, the first organization by and for American Negroes, was founded in Philadelphia by Absalom Jones and Richard Allen. Two years later, one of its branches in Newport, Rhode Island, "composed of twelve 'black gentlemen' who were 'Freeholders,' " made a proposal for "the return of Africans to Africa and the increase of friends who would promote their cause." The Philadelphia society decided that it was best to say little about this proposal, apparently because it was not in sympathy with it but did not wish to discourage those who might wish to return to Africa. One of the founders, Bishop Richard Allen of the newly formed African Methodist Episcopal Church, later came out against colonization in these words: "This land, which we have watered with our tears and our blood, is now our mother country; and we are well satisfied to stay where wisdom abounds and the Gospel is free." [2]

The first practical, if small-scale and short-lived, emigrationist effort was peculiarly influenced by British white colonizationism. In 1787, 332 "Black Poor," mainly men, were rounded up in the slums of London and transported to Sierra Leone, the British settlement on the west coast of Africa. Many of them were former American slaves freed by the British in return for service against the American revolutionary forces in the War for Independence and brought to England with the repatriated British soldiery.

In 1807 a private society, the African Institution, was established to help the British government in the management of the colony's trade and other affairs. The motives of its leaders and backers were mixed—to rid England of destitute and unwanted blacks; anti-slavery zeal; commercial profit; and Christian charity. The Quakers and missionary societies in general were particularly devoted to what was as much a cause as a colony.[3]

Sierra Leone had already attracted the favorable attention of two of the earliest white American colonizationists, Dr. William Thornton, a well-to-do Quaker physician, later appointed head of the United States Patent Office, and the Reverend Samuel D. Hopkins, pastor of the First Congregational Church in Newport, Rhode Island. From 1786 to 1790 Thornton worked at a plan to enable American Negroes to emigrate to Africa. Through his efforts, Negro societies were formed in Newport and Boston to which he spread the gospel of Sierra Leone. Two thousand Rhode Island Negroes expressed a desire to go to Africa when Thornton assured them that they would be set up as an independent nation (a term he used because he hated the word "colony").[4] That was as far as any of them were able to get. In 1789 Hopkins made inquiries about Sierra Leone on behalf of some Negro members of his congregation. In 1795 they sent a delegate there, and though he was offered some land, no one took advantage of it.[5] In 1800 a Negro slave revolt, known as "Gabriel's Conspiracy," broke out in Virginia. The Virginia legislature asked the federal government to look for some place out of the country to send the black insurgents. President Jefferson wrote to Governor James Monroe of Virginia that he preferred Africa and particularly called his attention to Sierra Leone. But the colony's authorities decided that they could not handle such an influx and declined the offer.[6]

One man finally did something about it. He was Paul Cuffe (or Cuffee), a prosperous sea captain, born on the island of Cuttyhunk, one of the Elizabeth Islands, off the coast of Massachusetts, of a Negro father and an American Indian mother. He went to sea at the age of sixteen and was perhaps the first Negro to own his own vessel. A Quaker, Cuffe heard about Sierra Leone in 1808 from a Philadelphia friend. He was invited to visit it and made his first trip in 1811. Then in his early fifties and owner or part owner of several ships, he was imbued with a sense of mission to "civilize" Africans with a transfusion of American Negroes and to help American Negroes by transporting some of them to Africa. In December 1815 he made a second trip to Sierra Leone, largely at his own expense, with thirty-eight Negro passengers, all common laborers who wanted to work on the land. The trip was so costly it convinced him that nothing much could be done without government support. Some of his passengers later wrote back, exhorting other American Negroes to follow their example: "Though you are free that is not your country. Africa, not America, is your country and your home." But by this time American Negro sentiment had turned against Africa. Curiously, for all the white agitation about sending Negroes back to Africa, Captain Cuffe was the only one to do anything about it until the Colonization Society went into the business. A one-shot operation, Cuffe's efforts represented a man more than a movement.[7]

Nevertheless, Cuffe was instrumental in getting other free Negroes interested in the work of the African Institution. Three of them, Daniel Coker, a teacher and missionary, James Forten, a wealthy sailmaker, and the Reverend Peter Williams, Jr., headed "miniature" African Institutions in Baltimore, Philadelphia, and New York, respectively.[8] The Americans, as Forten wrote to the British parent organization, considered themselves "as merely instruments for the furtherance of your views."[9] Thus, this incipient black "Back-to-Africa" campaign was primarily inspired by and tied to white British colonizationism. In turn, the Reverend Robert Finley turned to Captain Cuffe for advice before forming the American Colonization Society.

Once the Colonization Society was set up, its white auspices backfired on the black American appendages of the African Institution. Most free Negroes were affronted by the Society's efforts to send them to Africa, though emigration elsewhere did not immediately meet with the same disapproval. The efforts of the American version of the African Institution met with such widespread and militant opposition that its most influential sponsors found themselves isolated and rejected. In January 1817, James Forten was chairman of a meeting in Philadelphia to consider the advisability of protesting against the Colonization Society's plan "to exile us from the land of our nativity." Forten wrote sadly to Cuffe about the outcome: "We had a large meeting of Males at the Rev. R. Allens Church the other evening Three thousand at least attended and there was not one sole that was in favour of going to Africa. They think that the slave holders want to get rid of them so as to make their property more secure." After expressing the hope that the "Father of all mercies" might clear up the matter, Forten added regretfully: "We however have agreed to remain silent, as the people here both white & colour are decided against the measure." [10] The meeting unanimously adopted a resolution denouncing any effort "to banish us from her [America's] bosom" as not only cruel but "in direct violation of those principles, which have been the boast of this republic" and vowing that "we will never separate ourselves voluntarily from the slave population in this country." In August of the same year, the mass pressure on Forten was so great that he signed his name to a resolution which appealed to all the inhabitants of Philadelphia to join in opposition to African colonization, mainly on the ground that it would assure "perpetual slavery and augmented suffering." [11] By 1827 Forten and other free Negro leaders in Philadelphia and New York were so prejudiced against Africa that they called it "a land of destruction where the Sword will cut off the few wretched beings whom the climate spares." [12] By this time the British African Institution had exhausted its usefulness and had converted itself into nothing more than an anti-slavery society. It held its last public meeting in 1827, eking out a shadowy existence for a few more years.[13]

Thus the American offshoot of the African Institution did not get very far or last very long. Cuffe died in 1817. Forten was forced to join the anti-colonizationist opposition that same year. Coker soon gave up the struggle at home and took his own advice by going to Liberia on behalf of the American Colonization Society. The American-based African Institution and the American Colonization Society were so closely linked in the free Negroes' minds that only the latter could go on because it was promoted by whites.

In the 1820s most restless, dissatisfied free Negroes in the United States looked for escape toward Haiti or Canada. A few thousand—probably less than 10,000—emigrated to Haiti in the next two decades. Discrimination against free Negro laborers in Cincinnati, Ohio, at the end of the 1820s brought about an early exodus to Canada and led to the First National Negro Convention. To prevent skilled freed slaves from competing with white craftsmen, Cincinnati officials decided to enforce an old law requiring Negroes to post a bond guaranteeing good behavior and self-support. The bond was so high that it forced qualified Negroes to seek employment elsewhere. A delegation was sent to Canada to investigate the area bounded by Lakes Huron, Erie, and Ontario, and other Negro communities were asked to support those who wished to make the move from Cincinnati. This effort was one of the principal reasons for convening the first Negro convention in Philadelphia in June 1831. It voted to support those who wanted to move to Canada, but condemned emigration to Liberia as detrimental to the general welfare of the American Negro. About 2000 soon went to Canada, and perhaps as many as 10,000 in the next two decades. The enthusiasm for Haiti or Canada did not last long. By 1833 the Third National Negro Convention came out against emigration even to Canada except as a desperate expedient to escape from slavery.[14]

At this time, too, a significant change in terminology took place. In the seventeenth and eighteenth centuries American Negroes usually referred to themselves as "Africans" or "free Africans." In the first half of the nineteenth century they preferred to be known as "people of color" or the "colored population." The terms "Negroes" and "blacks" were also used but less frequently. "Negro" did not come into general usage until the nineteenth century, and it finally won out partly through the successful campaign led by Booker T. Washington to capitalize it. "Leaders among the freedmen felt that they might be told to 'go back to Africa' if they continued to call themselves 'African,'" Professor St. Clair Drake has written. "But they could not call themselves 'American,' for they had no fixed legal or customary status yet in the land of their birth. The gradual change in nomenclature was one aspect of the freedmen's insistence that they had a right to remain in America and to be recognized, eventually, as citizens. It also emphasized their determination to fight for the emancipation of those still enslaved rather than to become leaders, after emigration, in some black nation to be established overseas." [15] Thus the terms "colored" and "Negro" were stages of both Americanization and self-realization, despite a current myth that they were imposed by white men as a mark of Negro servitude or inferiority.*

* In 1928 Dr. W. E. B. Du Bois, then editor of *The Crisis,* organ of the National Association for the Advancement of Colored People, received a letter from a high-school sophomore who wanted to know why the magazine used the term "Negro," which he called "a white man's word to make us feel inferior."

Dr. Du Bois took the trouble to reply at length. He advised his young correspondent not to make the common error of "mistaking names for things" or that the name of a thing could be changed at will. Then he went on: "But why seek to change the name? 'Negro' is a fine word. Etymologically and phonetically it is much better and more logical than 'African' or 'colored' or any of the various hyphenated circumlocutions. Of course, it is not 'historically' accurate. No name ever was historically accurate: neither 'English,' 'French,' 'German,' 'White,' 'Jew,' 'Nordic' nor 'Anglo-Saxon.' They were all at first nicknames, misnomers, accidents, grown eventually to conventional habits and achieving accuracy because, and simply because, wide and continued usage rendered them accurate. In this sense 'Negro' is quite as accurate, quite as old and quite as definite as any name of any great group of people.

"Suppose now we could change the name. Suppose we arose tomorrow morning and lo! instead of being 'Negroes,' all the world called us 'Cheiropolidi'—do you really think this would make a vast and momentous difference to you and me? Would the Negro problem be suddenly and eternally settled? Would you be any less ashamed of being descended from a black man, or would your schoolmates feel any less superior to you? The feeling of inferiority is in you, not in any name. The name merely evokes what is already there. Exorcise the hateful complex and

Meanwhile, interest in emigration rose again in the 1840s. By the end of the decade it began to attract some of the best Negro minds of the period. One of them, Dr. Martin R. Delany, soon became the outstanding advocate of the new black nationalism, which almost invariably expressed itself in some form of emigrationist sentiment or scheme. The story of his life has been strangely neglected; not only is it worth telling for its own sake, but it is peculiarly symbolic of the entire course of black nationalism from the outset.

The extraordinary career of Dr. Delany demonstrated that it was not impossible for one whose face, it was said, "shone like black Italian marble" to achieve success in more than one field even in ante-bellum America—and yet to yearn for something else.

He was the grandson of slaves. His father's father was supposed to have been an African chieftain of the Golah tribe, captured with his family in battle, sold as slaves and brought to America. His mother's father was said to have been an African prince of the Mandingo line in the Niger Valley, also captured in war, enslaved, sold, transported to America. His parents, however, were free when he was born in Charleston, Virginia (now West Virginia), in 1812. He was taught how to read and write by itinerant Yankee peddlers who used to give free lessons as they sold the ubiquitous *New York Primer and Spelling Book*. When he was ten the household moved north to Chambersburg, Pennsylvania, ostensibly because his mother felt persecuted by white neighbors who resented the fact that her children were being taught to read. Nine years later he went off to Pittsburgh to attend a school run by a Negro educational society, his first serious opportu-

---

no name will ever make you hang your head." (*The Crisis,* March 1928, pp. 96–97.)

Yet times change, and now the term "Negro" has gone full circle. To show their contempt for the word black nationalists have gone back to the old form "negro" and capitalize "Black." See, for example, H. Rap Brown, *Die Nigger Die!* (New York: The Dial Press, 1969), p. 130.

nity to study. In 1843, when he was thirty-one, he began to put out in Pittsburgh one of the first Negro weekly publications, the *Mystery,* which he edited for almost four years. It was devoted to "the interest and elevation of his race," the cause with which he was increasingly identified, whatever else he was doing. In 1846 Frederick Douglass came to Pittsburgh and was so impressed with Delany's enterprise that they formed a temporary partnership. Delany disposed of his interest in the *Mystery* and, in 1847–48, served for a few months as Douglass's co-editor on the latter's first organ, the *North Star.* In 1849 Delany left Douglass altogether in favor of an earlier ambition, the study of medicine, and after being rejected by three schools, he was admitted into the Medical School of Harvard College, which he attended in 1851–1852. In his later practice he specialized in diseases of women and children.

At the age of forty Delany had proved his abilities in at least two professions. In his prime he was described as a formidable figure of a man. He was, his contemporary biographer wrote, of "medium height, compactly and strongly built, with broad shoulders, upon which rests a head seemingly inviting, by its bareness, attention to the well-developed organs, with eyes sharp and piercing, seeming to take in everything at a glance at the same time, while will, energy, and fire are alive in every feature; the whole surmounted on a groundwork of most defiant blackness." Delany himself liked to boast that "there lives none blacker than himself." Frederick Douglass is supposed to have said: "I thank God for making me a man simply; but Delany always thanks Him for making him a black man." [16] Another contemporary testified: "He is short, compactly built, has a quick, wiry walk, and is decided and energetic in conversation, unadulterated in race, and proud of his complexion. Though somewhat violent in his gestures, and paying but little regard to the strict rules of oratory, Dr. Delany is, nevertheless, an interesting, eloquent speaker." [17]

But journalism and medicine were merely prologue to Delany's historically more important political career. As late as 1851, it seems, he was still opposed to all emigrationism, even to Canada.[18] In 1852, however, he suddenly burst forth with a privately published book in which the earliest "black nationalism" was formulated in unmistakable terms and made him known as "the first major Negro nationalist" and "the embodiment of Negro separatism."[19] This book, *The Condition, Elevation, Emigration and Destiny of the Colored People of the United States,* and its even more famous Appendix, entitled "A Project for an Expedition of Adventure, to the Eastern Coast of Africa," constitute the *locus classicus* of black nationalism in America.

One sentence in the Appendix is the most quoted in the work: "We are a nation within a nation;—as the Poles in Russia, the Hungarians in Austria; the Welsh, Irish and Scotch in the British dominions." Therefore Delany advocated founding a new Negro nation on the eastern coast of Africa "for the settlement of colored adventurers from the United States and elsewhere."

But Delany's viewpoint and entire career were more complicated than these words might make him appear to be. A close reading of the entire book—neither the man nor his work has ever been given the study it deserves—reveals that his emigrationist nationalism sprang from a rather unusual source. In the body of the book Delany wrote: "Our common country is the United States. Here we were born, here raised and educated; here are the scenes of childhood; the pleasant associations of our school-going days; the loved enjoyments of our domestic and fireside relations, and the sacred graves of our departed fathers and mothers, and from here will we not be driven by any policy that may be schemed against us." He continued: "We are Americans, having a birthright citizenship—natural claims upon the country—claims common to all others of our fellow citizens—natural rights, which may, by virtue of unjust laws, be obstructed, but never can be annulled." Yet the Negroes were "aliens to the laws and political privileges of the country." Whatever the theory, the facts were "impregnable." In a later passage he expressed his attitude toward the United States even more poignantly: "We love our country, dearly love her, but she don't love us—she despises us, and bids us begone, driving us from her embraces. . . ." Thus Delany's "black nationalism" was based on unrequited love, on rejection by whites, rather than on a deeply rooted, traditional attachment to another soil and another nation.

In a letter that same year to William Lloyd Garrison, the leading white abolitionist, Delany clearly revealed that his pro-Africanism was a reluctant reaction to the refusal of whites to grant or accept full equality:

I am not in favor of caste, nor a separation of the brotherhood of mankind, and would as willingly live among white men as black, if I had an *equal possession and enjoyment* of privileges; but shall never be reconciled to live among them, subservient to their will—existing by mere *sufferance,* as we, the colored people, do, in this country. The majority of white men cannot see why colored men cannot be satisfied with their condition in Massachusetts—what they desire more than the *granted* right of citizenship. Blind selfishness on the one hand, and deep prejudice on the other, will not permit them to understand that we desire the *exercise* and *enjoyment* of these rights, as well as the *name* of their possession. If there were any probability of this, I should be willing to remain in the country, fighting and struggling on, the good fight of faith. But I must admit, that I have no hopes in this country—no confidence in the American people— with a *few* excellent exceptions—therefore, I have written as I have done [italics in original—T.D.].[20]

The only remedy, for Delany in 1852 and for some years thereafter, was mass emigration, which, he acknowledged, was "a new feature in our history." In the book itself he argued heatedly against going to Liberia and still wanted to stay at least in some part of the Americas: "Where shall we go? We must not leave this continent; America is our destination and our home." The only question was, North or South? He came down hard in favor of Central America, South America, and the West Indies. In another respect, however, his views anticipated those of Booker T. Washington. He advised his people that business was more important to them at that stage than the professions. "We should first be mechanics and common tradesmen, and professions as a matter of course would grow out of the wealth made thereby."

Thus Delany ruled out Africa in the body of the book. He added Africa to South America, Mexico, the West Indies, "etc.," only in the Appendix, without any explanation for his change of mind. By insisting on the eastern coast of Africa, about which he still knew little—he merely called for an expedition to find a suitable location for "colored adventurers," not necessarily for the entire people—he implied that he could not simply advocate that the American Negroes should go back to the African nation from which they had come. He hazily conceived of what was to be, in effect, a new nation somewhere in eastern Africa, a transplant from the United States. The entire scheme shows that he had hardly thought it out before he rushed into print. He wrote it hastily, as he himself related, in a month during a business trip to New York, while he was attending to other business during the day and sometimes lecturing on physiology in the evening. That he could turn out such a work in his spare time in so short a period was a tribute to his enormous energies, but the circumstances of its composition also explain some of its unevenness and discrepancies. The book itself encouraged emigration to the West Indies, South America or Central America; the Appendix encouraged emigration to Africa; and Delany made no effort to explain the shift in his interest.[21]

In any case the book was not "well received" by those for whom it was intended.[22] Abolitionists hotly criticized it as fostering another form of colonizationism and, therefore, acting as an impediment to immediate emancipation. Delany was sufficiently impressed by the criticism to order a halt in the sale of the book.[23] Thus, curiously, he owed his lasting fame to a hastily written book which he tried to suppress.

The pro-African Appendix was especially antipathetic to the American Negro mood, however emigrationist. In July 1853, when Delany and others issued a call for a National Emigration Convention to be held the following year, they warned that "no person will be admitted to a seat in the Convention, who would introduce the subject of emigration to the Eastern Hemisphere—either to Asia, Africa, or Europe —as our object and determination are to consider our claims to the West Indies, Central and South America, and the Canadas." [24] Inasmuch as Delany had come out in favor of all these places at one time or another, it was probably not too hard for him to agree to these terms. At the convention itself, held in Cleveland, August 24–26, 1854, Delany delivered a long report on the "Political Destiny of the Colored Race, on the American Continent," in which he forecast that Canada was destined to come into the United States "at no very distant day" and therefore recommended the former as a "temporary asylum" only. He strongly favored emigration to Central America, South America, and the West Indies, with Canada as a last resort if it remained independent and if the other places proved to be unfeasible. The action of the convention itself, however, was much more cautious. It merely passed a resolution urging American Negroes to purchase as much land as possible in Canada, especially in the still sparsely settled western provinces, without making any reference to land south of the United States.[25] It authorized a "foreign mission" to make a "geographical, topographical and political" survey of such countries as it might choose, with the proviso that "the position of the colored people in the United States be not compromised." And it adopted a "Platform: or Declaration of Sentiments" which indicated a much greater interest in equality in the United States than emigration elsewhere.[26]

Subsequently Delany revealed that the convention had not altogether neglected Africa. In "secret sessions," he disclosed, the convention had agreed to hold Africa *"in reserve."* [27] For the time being, however, emigrationist hopes centered on Haiti. In 1855 the Reverend James Theodore Holly went to Haiti for a month and reported that laborers were offered "favorable inducements" to settle there.[28] A second emigrationist convention was held in 1856, by which time Delany had moved to Chatham, Ontario, one of the organized Negro communities in Canada, and illness prevented him from attending. Finally, at the third convention, held at Chatham in 1858, Delany's wish was granted. He was permitted to head an expedition of five "to make a topographical, geological and geographical examination of the Valley of the River Niger." But his commission explicitly stipulated that the expedition was for "the purposes of science and for general information; and without any reference to, and with the [General] Board [of Commissioners] being entirely opposed to any Emigration there as such." [29] This was hardly evidence of backing for his more far-reaching scheme. Delany set off for Africa in 1859; he traveled widely for about a year, during which he signed "treaties" with eight native kings of Abeokuta for grants of land to establish American Negro colonies in the Yoruba area. Soon afterward the kings "reneged on" the grants.[30]

While Delany was in New York arranging for his trip to Africa, he showed the manuscript of a novel, *Blake: or, the Huts of America,* to the editors of the forthcoming *Anglo-African Magazine.* He permitted them to copy Chapters 28, 29, and 30 only, which they proceeded to publish in the first number, dated January 1859. Then he evidently changed his mind because the magazine went back to Chapter 1 in the next issue and continued to publish the first twenty-three chapters in the subsequent six issues, whereupon it suddenly cut off further installments without explanation. So we will never know how the story came out, except for the information in an editorial note that the entire work contained some eighty chapters and about six hundred pages and "not only shows the combined political and commercial interests that unite the North and South, but gives in the most familiar manner the formidable understanding among the slaves in the United States and Cuba." The hero of the story is Henry, "a black—a pure negro—handsome, manly and intelligent," who had been educated in the West Indies but "decoyed away" into slavery in Mississippi in his youth. When Henry learned that his wife had been sold and sent off to Cuba during his absence, he decided to organize a secret movement of slaves throughout the South to set off a "general insurrection." Most of the published chapters tell how he went from state to state organizing the uprising. Delany was no novelist, but he was willing to try his hand at almost anything (including a "new theory" of planetary attraction), and his novel can be read with much profit as a fascinating political and social document.[31]

From Africa, Delany in 1860 went on to London—where a highly revealing international incident occurred. His exploration of Africa had made him something of a celebrity, and he was invited to attend the International Statistical Congress in July of that year, an honor which he particularly savored. It was a most distinguished gathering of scientists from all over the world, and the entire diplomatic corps, including the American Ambassador, George Mifflin Dallas, a former Vice-President of the United States, was present. After an opening address by Prince Albert, the royal consort, some special guests were introduced by the eighty-two-year-old Lord Brougham, the eminent British legal reformer, well known for his anti-slavery sentiments. According to the account in *The Times* of London, Lord Brougham ended his introductions by turning to the American Ambassador and saying: "I hope our friend Mr. Dallas will forgive me reminding him that there is a negro present, a member of the Congress." *The Times* reported that this statement was greeted with "loud laughter and vociferous cheering." Inasmuch as the others had responded to Lord Brougham's introductions, Delany decided to say a few words: "I pray your Royal Highness will allow me to thank his lordship, who is always a most unflinching friend of the negro, and I assure your Royal Highness and his lordship that I am a man." This pointed remark, which suggested that there were places where Delany was not treated as "a man," was not lost on the audience. *The Times* noted: "This novel and unexpected incident elicited a round of cheering very extraordinary for an assemblage of sedate statisticians." [32]

Ambassador Dallas, a native of Philadelphia, was stunned by the unexpected scene. He described his reaction in his diary:

I perceived instantly the grossness of the act, and seeing the black in the very centre of the philosophers, hadn't a doubt that it was a premeditated contrivance to provoke me into some unseemly altercation with the coloured personage. I balked that by remaining silent and composed. The gentleman of colour, however, rose, and requested permission of the Prince Consort, as chairman, to thank Lord Brougham for his notice, with an emphatic conclusion, "I am a man." Query: Is not the [British] government answerable for this insult? Or must it be regarded as purely the personal indecency of Lord Brougham? [33]

The official American delegate to the Congress, Judge Augustus Baldwin Longstreet, then President of South Carolina College, was much less composed. His biographer has recorded: "Longstreet, taking all this for a deliberate reflection upon both him and his government, from that contaminate assemblage withdrew his presence. Brougham's action, he reported to the Secretary of the Treasury, had constituted 'an

ill-timed assault upon our country, a wanton indignity offered to our minister, and a pointed insult offered to me.'
There was great commotion." [34] With the exception of one
delegate from Boston, who represented his state only, the entire American delegation strode out of the Congress in protest. Judge Longstreet later explained that his withdrawal
had been provoked less by the remarks of Lord Brougham or
Dr. Delany than by the demonstrative response of the entire
assembly.[35] The following day Lord Brougham only made
matters worse by trying to explain his "offense." He protested: "Why, here we see in this unequalled council, a son
of Africa, one of that race whom we have been taught to look
upon as inferior. I only alluded to this as one of the most
gratifying as well as extraordinary facts of the age." [36] Both
Lord Brougham and the philanthropic Lord Shaftesbury
made efforts to mollify the American Ambassador publicly
and privately, without success.

The British and American press sizzled over the contre-
temps for days. The British papers professed to be shocked
by the American walkout. The American press, even in New
York, was divided. *The Evening Post* and *The New York
Tribune* sided with Lord Brougham. The former commented
caustically:

> Under ordinary circumstances and if addressed to any other
> man in the assembly, such a remark would have had no sig-
> nificance, but addressed to the representative of the Amer-
> ican government, which denies to the negro the privilege of
> citizenship or the capacity to acquire it, addressed to Mr.
> Dallas, who refuses colored people wishing to visit the Old
> World the protection of his country's flag, the simple testi-
> monial of a passport that they are Americans, the remark of
> Lord Brougham was certainly one of the most humiliating
> public rebukes ever administered by one statesman to
> another.

The Tribune interpreted the incident as showing "the scorn
with which an enlightened and unprejudiced people look

upon proscription on account of color put in force by a nation whose unceasing boast is of the perfect freedom it secures to all." But three papers were lined up on the other side. *The World* accused Lord Brougham of a "constitutional *penchant* for snubbing foreign ministers." *The New York Times* held that Lord Brougham had convicted himself "of a violation of Parliamentary rules, scarcely to be expected from one of his years and experience, but also of a decided breach of common politeness." And *The New York Herald* was so wrathful that it turned in rage on the American Ambassador: "The conduct of Mr. Dallas, the Minister of the United States in England, in not resenting the insulting sneer addressed to him, in his capacity as the representative of his country and its institutions, by Lord Brougham, at the meeting of the Statistical Congress of all nations, is deserving of the severest reprobation at the hands of the American people and the American government." [37]

The only one who came out of this imbroglio unscathed was Dr. Delany himself. Before leaving London, he read a paper on his researches in Africa before the Royal Geographical Society. He continued to lecture on Africa in England and Scotland for almost seven months. He returned to Canada in 1861, six weeks after the Civil War had broken out, and then went to the United States for more lectures. He had, by this time, spent almost ten years in propaganda and organization to convince his compatriots to leave the country and settle elsewhere, preferably in Africa. None of his efforts had produced the slightest practical result. In 1861–62 several hundred Negroes did emigrate from the United States and Canada to Haiti, but that was largely the work of the Reverend Holly. Unfavorable circumstances and the war quickly aborted this experiment, and most of the emigrants were soon glad to return north. As late as 1862, 242 California Negroes sent a petition to Congress to colonize them "in some country in which their color will not be a badge of degradation." They preferred to go anywhere than to stay in the United

States, where, they said, Negroes faced a dismal, if not a hopeless, future. But this group was exceptional; the Civil War was itself the great hope of the vast majority of American Negroes.[38] For Delany, the Civil War was, in a sense, a test of his emigrationist beliefs. If he really felt that Negroes were "aliens" in the United States, North and South, the victory of one side or the other should not have mattered so much to him. Even if his sympathies almost inevitably went out to the North, his emigrationist position did not logically oblige him to support it, and he might even have said a plague on both their houses.

Yet, according to the biography written in his own lifetime, Delany soon said that the war "had become inseparable from his daily existence, almost absorbing everything else, and nothing would content him but entering the service; he cared not how, provided his admission recognized the rights of his race to do so." [39] He wanted to organize what he called a "corps d'Afrique," that is, a totally black unit in the Union Army. Determined to get into the action, he obtained an appointment as acting assistant agent for recruiting and acting examining surgeon in Chicago. He then recruited in Massachusetts, Rhode Island, Pennsylvania, New York, Ohio, and Connecticut. He co-authored a letter to Secretary of War Edwin M. Stanton, offering to raise "a regiment or brigade in a shorter time than could otherwise be effected." [40] Early in 1865, the last year of the war, he managed to confer with President Lincoln personally.

As Delany later told the story, it was a historic encounter. With "a generous grasp and shake of the hand," Lincoln led Delany to a seat in front of him. "Serious without sadness, and pleasant withal," Delany recalled, the President placed himself "at ease, the better to give me a patient audience."

Lincoln made the first move. "What can I do for you, sir?"

"Nothing, Mr. President," Delany replied proudly. "But I've come to propose something to you, which I think will be beneficial to the nation in this critical hour of her need."

They talked frankly about the prejudices that prevented white soldiers from serving under a black commander or white officers from associating with black officers. When Lincoln asked Delany how he would "remedy" this condition, the latter launched into his grand design:

> I propose, sir, an army of blacks, commanded entirely by black officers, except such whites as may volunteer to serve; this army to penetrate through the heart of the South, and make conquests, with the banner of Emancipation unfurled, proclaiming freedom as they go, sustaining and protecting it by arming the emancipated, taking them as fresh troops, and leaving a few veterans among the new freedmen, when occasion requires, keeping this banner unfurled until every slave is free, according to the letter of your proclamation.

Delany promised an army of 40,000 blacks in three months.

Lincoln was delighted. "This is the very thing I have been looking and hoping for; but nobody offered it." He chided Delany that the latter had not understood his Proclamation and had previously advised remaining passive in order not to embarrass or compromise the government. Then the President suddenly turned and said: "Will you take command?" A few minutes later he handed him a card of introduction to Secretary Stanton on which was written: "Do not fail to have an interview with this most extraordinary and intelligent black man." [41]

Delany was soon commissioned a Major of Infantry, attached to the 104th United States Colored Troops—which was much better than Frederick Douglass, who also wanted a commission, was able to do.[42] Major Delany was sent to Charleston, South Carolina, to aid in the recruitment and organization of another Negro regiment. To his pious biographer, and no doubt to most Negroes at that time, Delany the Major of Infantry was far more important than Delany the father of emigrationism.

After the Civil War, Delany settled in Charleston, where he began a new—and still more surprising—career.

South Carolina in 1865 was a burned-out shell. Its Negroes had been freed, but little else had been done for them or even decided. The Freedmen's Bureau was set up in March of that year, mainly to give them aid and protect their interests. In this bureau, Major Delany—he was no longer called "Doctor"—worked for the next three years. This position, his military rank, and the prestige he had brought with him from the North enabled him to play an increasingly active part in the political life of the state. When the question of Negro suffrage arose, Delany did not hesitate to write to President Andrew Johnson, whom he assured that the blacks were a new force in American life, without which the Civil War could not have been won. "What becomes necessary, then, to secure and perpetuate the Union," he argued, "is simply the *enfranchisement* and recognition of the *political equality* of the blacks with the whites in all of their relations as American citizens." [43] He participated in a Colored People's Convention at Charleston in November 1865, the first organized effort of South Carolina Negro leaders to act together politically. The convention, which referred to itself as "an extraordinary meeting, unknown in the history of South Carolina," demanded equal suffrage and all other rights of citizenship for Negroes.[44] The emphasis was all on equality at home, not emigration abroad. Delany's influence must have been considerable, even if Longstreet's biographer no doubt exaggerated by attributing to Delany "practical control of Charleston, holding it under his foot, revelling in his enjoyment of newly gained authority." [45] As late as 1924, when the Longstreet biography was published, it was still possible to perpetuate in print the affronts and aspersions which Delany must have suffered in his time.

After the Freedmen's Bureau, Delany spent several years as a custom-house inspector at Charleston. During these years, in the late 1860s and early 1870s, South Carolina politics were dominated by the Radical Republicans, based largely on Negro support. In 1874, however, a split in the Radical Party gave Delany his greatest political opportunity. A newly formed Independent Radical Party nominated a white judge, John T. Green, for governor, and Delany for lieutenant-governor. Delany campaigned so ably that former Governor Benjamin F. Perry, not a friend of Negro political rights, paid him this tribute: "I must say he has exhibited, in his speeches and addresses, more wisdom and prudence, more honor and patriotism, than any other Republican in South Carolina, white or black." [46] A major South Carolina historian, referring to this period, paid tribute to Delany as "the upright and able Negro." [47] Green and Delany were narrowly defeated by a vote of 80,403 to 68,818. Green died a few months later, and historians have noted that, if Green had been elected, "Delany would have become governor largely through the vote of white people." [48] For one who had been in the state no more than ten years, and whom many whites thought of as a "Negro carpetbagger," even if of "the best type," [49] this was no small achievement.

The Democratic Party made its comeback in South Carolina in 1876. As the political instrument of the pre-Civil War slave-holding white oligarchy, it was abominated by most Negroes. The man who enabled the Democrats to regain power was Wade Hampton, a former Confederate general and wealthy planter. In his campaign Hampton used what friendly historians have called "force without violence" [50] to intimidate the Negroes and friendly persuasion to win them over. His "force" was made up of armed whites organized into "rifle clubs," whose uniform was a red shirt. These "Red Shirts," as they were called, "were used for political purposes and the display of armed force intimidated many voters," historians have testified.[51] Hampton also appealed to Negroes to support him as their best Democratic friend. There were no Negroes at the convention that nominated Hampton and none on the Democratic ticket, despite a substantial majority of Negro voters in the state.

To the astonishment and consternation of most South Carolina Negroes, Delany came out for Hampton and campaigned vigorously for him. Delany was not the only Negro to support the Democrats, but the vast majority remained loyal to the Republicans. His position was so little appreciated by most Negroes that Delany was treated roughly. At one meeting he was "howled down" and prevented from finishing his speech.[52] Another incident, known as the "Cainhoy massacre," was more serious. A riot broke out at a meeting near Cainhoy, in Charleston County, at which Delany was again prevented from speaking; he and others were forced to take refuge in a brick house adjoining the local church, which was attacked by infuriated Negroes armed with muskets; six whites and one Negro were killed that day in battles that raged in and around the town.[53] But Delany went on campaigning for Hampton, who gained enough Negro votes to win the election.[54] The vote was so close that only a few Negro votes were needed to tip the balance. Hampton promptly rewarded Delany by appointing him a trial justice in Charleston.

Why did Delany turn against the Negro Reconstructionists and go over to Wade Hampton, whom they considered their white enemy? In 1867, two years after the end of the Civil War, Delany had urged Negroes to "be satisfied to take things like other men in their natural course and time, preparing themselves in every particular for local municipal positions," and then they could "expect to attain to some others in time." But most Negro leaders in South Carolina were not satisfied to wait for what they considered their due share of power. By 1870, 86 of the 156 members of the state legislature were Negroes, and the Negro majority rose to 106 two years later. Delany himself continued to be more interested in "public equality" than in "social equality." The former consisted of full civil and political rights as well as free access to most public facilities. "Social equality," Delany thought, could not be legislated. "I don't believe in social equality; there is no such thing," he told a large Charleston audience in 1870. "If we want to associate with a man, we'll do it, and without laws." In that same year, however, his own ambitions rose, and he contended that "black men must have black leaders," including "a colored Lieutenant-Governor, and two colored men in the House of Representatives and one in the Senate, and our quota of State and county officers." [55] In 1871, however, Delany sternly censured the "carpetbaggers" from the North, some of whom worked for the Freedmen's Bureau, for deliberately dividing colored people and accused them of "deception, lying, cheating and stealing." He scoffed at them as generally coming from the "lowest grade of Northern society, Negro haters at home . . . who could not have been elected to any position of honor or trust in their homes." [56] With such sentiments Delany earned a reputation as one of the more moderate Negro spokesmen in the state.

In a letter to Justice J. J. Wright, a Negro, in 1874, before Delany was nominated for lieutenant-governor, he criticized the Reconstructionists so severely that he ascribed to them only one commendable act. This was the establishment of a Land Commission, set up to buy lands and distribute them to freedmen, but fraud and corruption had largely defeated its purpose. In his letter Delany blamed the Reconstructionists for excessive taxation and cautioned the Negroes against corruption. Though blacks outnumbered whites in the state at this time, he foresaw with foreboding a future white majority through increased immigration. "The white race," he wrote, "is true to itself, and it is useless and doing injustice to both races to conceal the fact that in giving liberty and equality of right to the blacks, they had no desire to see them rule over their own race." And he added: "Rest assured of this that there are no white people North or South, who will submit to see the black rule over the whites in America." [57]

Delany's position commended him to the state press, which frequently praised him as "the honest exemplar of the honest colored men of South Carolina." Most of the white press supported Delany's candidacy in 1874, as a result of which he and Judge Green won the moderate white vote.[58] In 1876 Delany supported Hampton, then regarded as a proponent of compromise, on the ground that it was necessary "to aid that effort which tends to bring about a union of the two races . . . in one common interest in the State." [59] A newspaper reporter noted that Delany was quickly forgiven for his support of Hampton. "Negroes who would have smashed his skull gleefully in September, 1876, were going to him in 1878 with their troubles and obeyed without question his orders, advice and interpretations of the law. What he said was law and he straightened the most complicated domestic relations happily and justly. White people also learned to respect him and trust him implicitly." [60]

Nevertheless, Delany's last important political act was to give aid and comfort to what one historian has called a white "counter-revolution." [61] By the end of the century, few Negroes even had the right to vote in South Carolina. Delany seems to have had no regrets. While serving as trial justice, he was visited by a British traveler, Sir George Campbell, who left this impression:

> I went to see Mr. D——, a pure negro and notable character. He has been in England and in Africa, and has seen the world. He is now a justice of the peace here—Trial Justice, they call it. He was appointed by Wade Hampton. He seems a very characteristic, pleasant, amusing sort of person, and talks well. He was educated in the North. He is in favour of Wade Hampton, who, he says, appoints black men when they are really educated and fit. I hear he quite holds his own as a justice.[62]

The old Delany was not totally suppressed. During his term as trial justice there was a mass agitation for a Negro exodus from South Carolina, partially set off by Hampton's election.

In 1878 a boat chartered by the Liberian Exodus Association carried 206 passengers from Charleston to Liberia. Despite the harsh things he had written about Liberia in his 1852 book, Delany was drawn into the movement, which, as always, ended disastrously.[63] Of this campaign, Sir George Campbell commented shrewdly: "The upper class of blacks do not go themselves, but preach to their countrymen the advantage of going." [64] In these hectic years Delany somehow found time to apply for a patent on an invention to facilitate the ascent and descent of locomotives.[65]

But Delany had hitched his wagon to Wade Hampton, whose governorship did not last very long. In 1878 the Republican extremists, who considered him much too soft on the Negro question, succeeded in ridding themselves of him in state politics by sending him to the United States Senate. With Hampton gone, Delany was soon deprived of his influential judicial post. "I lost as soon as they got rid of him [Hampton] by sending him to the U.S. Senate, as he was too liberal for the rank and file of the party leaders," Delany commented ruefully.[66] In 1879 Delany had the satisfaction of publishing a book on "ethnology." In it, he argued in favor of keeping the races "pure" by discouraging intermarriage, and he forecast that in time "there will be but the three original sterling races"—yellow, black, and white. The "African race in Africa," he admonished, should not be judged "by those portions of that race found out of Africa," whom he considered vastly inferior to those in Africa. His last thoughts on Africa were: "Untrammelled in its native purity, the race is a noble one, and worthy to emulate the noble Caucasian and Anglo-Saxon, now at the top round of the ladder of moral and intellectual grandeur in the progress of civilization." But he held that "the regeneration of the African race can only be effected by its own efforts, the efforts of its own self, whatever aid may come from other sources." [67]

Delany returned to the practice of medicine, but soon

moved to Boston, where he was employed by a mercantile house as an agent for a Central American firm. He died in January 1885 at the age of seventy-three in Xenia, Ohio.

Such in brief was the extraordinary life of the founding father of black nationalism in America. Yet the consistently emigrationist portion of his life filled only about ten years. After 1861 he went further and further away from the cause to which he owes his fame, and for almost a quarter of a century he represented reconciliation far more than emigration. His entire life was filled with contradictions and dualities. Before the Civil War his achievements would have done honor to any man, white or black. Yet the fact that Delany was black made it possible for one of his superior gifts and attainments to advocate fleeing from the land of his birth. Whatever his rank or profession, he still felt despised and rejected. But this was only one side of the story, the side that black nationalists have preferred to remember. The other side was that he never fled very far from home, and even his sojourn in Canada did not last long. He went to Africa as an explorer, not as a settler. Once the Civil War offered some hope of emancipation, he could not restrain his impulse to throw himself into the thick of it. Then he more or less made peace with the country that he once said had bade him begone and had driven him from her embraces. He preferred to support a moderate white, Wade Hampton, than to go all the way with the extreme black Reconstructionists, and thus indirectly helped to restore white rule in South Carolina. This was the final contradiction, the ultimate duality, in the life and public services of Martin R. Delany.

What explains the contradictions and dualities in Delany's thinking and behavior? The answer may give us some insight into the motivation for a nascent black nationalism from Delany's time to the present. As we have seen, Delany would infinitely have preferred freedom and equality in the United States. In this respect, there was not so much

difference in principle between himself and those who rejected emigrationism. Both preferred, if they could get it,
full American nationalism. The non-American or even anti-
American nationalist impulse was rooted in frustration and
despair, not in a natural, inevitable allegiance to another
country.

Thus emigration was far more a negative reaction than a
positive identification. The emigrationists themselves could
disagree on which country was best for their purposes—
somewhere in Africa, Haiti, Mexico, or elsewhere—because
no other country could claim to be their native land. Delany
himself could advocate emigration to Africa, move to Canada
for a few years, come back to the United States for the rest
of his life, and retain his interest in emigration for the less
fortunate. Delany's emigrationism was clearly related to his
notion of a "nation within a nation." But if the American
Negroes were truly a "nation within a nation," they would
have had to seek national self-determination where they
were—in some sense, inside the white nation—and not by
removing themselves from their native habitat. Delany was
never able to face this dilemma, and therefore he was neither
successful in persuading his fellow black Americans nor consistent in the way he ordered his own life.

Thus emigrationism from the outset reflected the dual
nature, the halfway house, of what might better be thought
of as a quasi-nationalism. This quasi-nationalism had its
roots not only in the "peculiar institution" that was slavery
but in the "peculiar institution" that was freedom for the
Negro. Paradoxically, then, black nationalism in America
arose out of a frustrated American nationalism, and the
frustration could only take quasi-nationalist forms.

This unresolved problem haunted all the emigrationists
of the nineteenth century. They were men who deserve the
highest respect and admiration for their struggles with a

recalcitrant reality, and if they never succeeded in making their program popular and viable, it was basically not their fault.

Even the most ardent emigrationists were not naïve enough to believe that emigration was a practical solution for the American Negro population as a whole. At best it might be the salvation for some, perhaps in time for a considerable number, but still far short of even a majority of a black American population that increased from about 5,000,000 in 1870 to about 9,000,000 in 1900.

The Reverend Henry Highland Garnet, another great Negro abolitionist and rival of Frederick Douglass, at first argued against African emigration. In 1848 he maintained: "We are planted here, and we cannot as a whole people, be re-colonized back to our fatherland. It is too late to make a successful attempt to separate the black and white people in the New World." Despite his profound grievances and disappointments, he went on: "America is my home, my country, and I have no other. I love whatever good there may be in her institutions. I hate her sins. I loathe her slavery, and I pray Heaven that ere long she may wash away her guilt in tears of repentance." [68]

In 1858, however, he was largely instrumental in founding the African Civilization Society for "the civilization and christianization of Africa" and of African descendants everywhere. Three years later, after meeting with the indefatigable Dr. Delany, the society decided to take a position on the vexed question of emigration. It went only part of the way: "The Society is not designed to encourage general emigration, but will aid only such persons as may be practically qualified." [69] Garnet himself did not get to Africa, which had become the land where he wanted to die, until 1881, when he was appointed Minister to Liberia. He died only two months after reaching his post.[70]

The Reverend James Theodore Holly, the leading advocate of emigration to Haiti, was no less candid. He called for "a select, judicious and discreet" emigration, not an "indiscriminate and *en masse* emigration pouring upon the shores of Hayti," which he thought would do more harm than good. He wanted no more than "limited debarkation on her [Haiti's] shores at appropriate intervals; and a mighty and headlong rush of emigrants must be avoided and discouraged by every possible means." [71] How at this rate the Negro population could be completely removed from the United States, he did not explain.

The fire-eating Bishop Henry M. Turner, who carried on the emigrationist tradition in the second half of the nineteenth century, was equally clear on this point. He disclaimed the idea that millions of poor black Americans could be assimilated by Africa. "Such a course would be madness in the extreme and folly unpardonable," he explained. "Five or ten thousand a year would be enough." For all his militant emigrationism, he protested: "All this jargon about 'Bishop Turner trying to get all us colored people out of the United States' is not only nonsense, but absolutely false, for two-thirds of the American Negroes would be of no help to anyone anywhere." [72] On another occasion, Bishop Turner called for the return of two or three million,[73] but at the rate of five or ten thousand a year, this would have taken at least two to three hundred years.

In any case, "African fever" flared up again toward the end of the century. An African Emigration Association was established in 1881 and, five years later, asked Congress for an appropriation to enable "thousands of us in humble circumstances" to return to Africa "and there try to build up a United States in Africa, modeled after this Government, and under the protecting care of the same, for the elevation of the African and for the perpetuity of our race, which is here losing its identity by intermixture with the white races, and other troubles." [74] Bishop Turner, who also thought that the American government should pay for the transportation to Africa, went to the trouble of calculating that the

United States owed the ex-slaves forty billion dollars, which he broke down to one hundred dollars a year for two million persons for two hundred years. The only white politicians sympathetic to this scheme were unreconstructed Southerners. In 1890, several bills were introduced in Congress to provide federal funds to pay for the Negroes' transportation to Africa, including one by Senator Matthew Butler of South Carolina which called for five million dollars, and another by Senator John T. Morgan of Alabama, who favored the Congo. These bills were ridiculed or denounced by almost the entire Negro press and never even came to a vote. "All this native land talk is nonsense," scoffed Frederick Douglass in 1894. "The native land of the American Negro is America." [75] Douglass had held this position for almost half a century.* But Bishop Turner knew who his real

---

* It is worth recalling Douglass's classical profession of faith as far back as November 16, 1849, in the *North Star*: "We deem it a settled point that the destiny of the colored man is bound up with that of the white people of this country; be the destiny of the latter what it may. It is idle—worse than idle, ever to think of our expatriation, or removal. The history of the colonization society must extinguish all such speculations. We are rapidly filling up the number of four millions; and all the gold of California combined, would be insufficient to defray the expenses attending our colonization. We are, as laborers, too essential to the interests of our white fellow-countrymen, to make a very grand effort to drive us from this country among probable events. While labor is needed, the laborer cannot fail to be valued; and although passion and prejudice may sometimes vociferate against us, and demand our expulsion, such efforts will only be spasmodic, and can never prevail against the sober second thought of self-interest. *We are here,* and here we are likely to be. To imagine that we shall ever be eradicated is absurd and ridiculous. We can be remodified, changed, and assimilated, but never extinguished. We repeat, therefore, that *we are here;* and that this is *our* country; and the question for philosophers and statesmen of the land ought to be, What principles should dictate the policy of the action towards us? We shall neither die out, nor be driven out; but shall go with this people, either as a testimony against them, or as an evidence in their favor throughout their generations. We are clearly on their hands, and must remain there for ever. All this we say for the benefit of those who hate the Negro more than they love their country." (Philip S. Foner, ed., *The Life and Writings of Frederick Douglass* [New York: International Publishers, 1951–52], I, 417; italics in original.)

allies were and enthusiastically backed Senators Butler and Morgan. Yet he again felt it necessary to explain that Senator Butler's bill did not require all American blacks to move to Africa. "Thousands and hundreds of thousands of us are no more fit to go to Africa than we are fit to go to Paradise," he explained.[76]

As far as Africa was concerned, he was soon corroborated by events. In 1894, Bishop Turner's pro-African propaganda inspired some white Southerners to organize an International Migration Society to transport Negroes, for a fee, to Liberia. With Bishop Turner's backing and despite much black opposition, the society managed to send off one ship with 197 black emigrants in 1895 and another with 321 in 1896. They went to Liberia with exaggerated hopes; the country was not prepared to receive them; a few stayed and made good; most regretted the move almost as soon as they arrived, suffered, and died or made their way back to the United States.[77] In 1894 also, a Mexican Colonization Society was formed by a wealthy Mexican who wanted cheap American Negro labor to pick cotton. It succeeded in inducing approximately 816 Negro farm laborers from Alabama to move the following year. This experiment also ended, as its historian put it, "in complete and tragic failure," and only about one-half of the emigrants were able to get back home safely.[78]

What was wrong? As the able historian of Bishop Turner's period has pointed out, Africa lured just those poor, desperate "black peasants" whom Africa needed and wanted the least.[79] Those black Americans with the most education, greatest professional skills, and highest standards of living needed and wanted Africa the least. Emigrationism was never able to overcome this social contradiction. The quasi-nationalism which it represented never had much of a chance because it did not appeal to the Negro middle class, which alone had the money, organization, and skills to make it profitable for both the emigrant and the country which received him. It is useless to blame the Negro middle class for refusing to emigrate *en masse*; the trouble must be sought in the conditions, both in America and in Africa, which made emigration so unattractive to those most capable of making a success of it.

How, then, could emigrationists hope to solve the American Negro problem if relatively few American Negroes wanted to emigrate and those who did emigrate were doomed to failure? A final argument occurred to both Bishop Holly and Bishop Turner. In 1859, the former maintained that the "African race" throughout the world, including the United States, was exploited and oppressed "simply because there is no powerful and enlightened negro nationality anywhere existing to espouse the cause and avenge the wrongs of their race." The lack of such a nationality, he believed, was "the potent cause of all the wrongs that the negro race now suffers under in the world." If only such a nationality could be established, he asserted, its influence would be "all-powerful in shielding and protecting each individual of the race, in which such a nationality inheres, no matter how humble that individual may be." But he insisted on a crucial condition: "We do not simply want a *negro nationality,* but we want a *strong, powerful, enlightened and progressive negro nationality, equal to the demands of the nineteenth century, and capable of commanding the respect of all the nations of the earth,* in order to exert in an effectual manner this reflex influence" (italics in original). Holly contended that Haiti was "the most favorably situated to be brought up to the required standpoint of modern civilization."[80] In 1883, Turner resorted to much the same reasoning, mainly on behalf of Liberia. He extolled the need for a black state "that the world will respect and [whose] glory and influence will tell upon the destinies of the race from pole to pole; our children's children can rest securely under

[its] aegis, whether in Africa, Europe, Asia, America or upon the high seas." [81]

This line of reasoning presupposed that black Americans were socially and economically superior to the people of the existing black nations such as Haiti or Liberia. With a Haitian population of only about one million in 1859 and a Liberian population of probably less than a million in 1883, Holly and Turner could hope to achieve their aims with a relatively restricted, selective black American emigration. In effect, black Americans were supposed to help Haiti or Liberia become strong, powerful, enlightened, and progressive in order for Haiti or Liberia to irradiate its influence to save all black Americans. At best this theory presupposed the considerable emigration of just those black Americans least likely to go, and those who did go were least likely to endear themselves to the backward natives who were then expected to shield and protect them. Bishop Holly and Bishop Turner were not the last to think of this far-fetched rationale to make some form of emigrationism palatable to black Americans. It has been hard for their successors to think of anything fundamentally new.

Delany, Bishop Turner, Edward W. Blyden, H. Ford Douglass, the Reverend Henry Highland Garnet, and a few others have become the heroes and prophets of today's black nationalism.[82] Even Frederick Douglass is being denigrated as a kind of Uncle Tom because he opposed this trend. In their own time, however, relatively few Negroes took Delany or Turner very seriously and even fewer acted on their advice. The historical problem is not merely why they advocated going back to Africa but why their efforts came to so little.

From Pan-Africa
to Back-to-Africa

3

Colonization and emigration were two sides of the same coin. If one was a white fantasy, the other was no less a fantasy because it was black. Yet this fantasy is so deeply rooted that it continued—and continues—to take numerous, extremely variegated forms.

One subtle intellectual expression was represented by a truly outstanding figure of the present century, Dr. W. E. B. Du Bois. In 1897 he first projected the idea that American Negroes were Americans—by birth, citizenship, political ideals, language, and religion. But whatever was unique in the American Negroes, he contended, was tied up with the entire Negro world outside America—with "Pan-Negroism." [1]

In effect, Du Bois joined together the two strains that had been struggling for supremacy among American Negroes. They were, he maintained, neither American nor African but something of both. Du Bois thus opened himself to attack from both camps, from those who utterly rejected their African past and those who bitterly rejected their American present. But Du Bois never succeeded in reconciling the two forces; he held them in an extremely uneasy and unstable equilibrium, which he himself could not always control.

Du Bois's "double-consciousness" of being both an American and a Negro led him a quarter of a century later to the espousal of a Pan-African movement in which he called on American Negroes to play a leading role. Du Bois devoted about a decade of his long and prolific career to this work, mainly in the form of Pan-African Congresses, of which four were held between 1919 and 1927, and a fifth and last in 1945. Pan-Africanism for Du Bois did not mean Negro separation from the United States; rather it implied American Negro leadership of the cause and interests of Negroes throughout the world, especially in Africa, which was still largely dominated by white imperialisms. In his voluminous works Dr. Du Bois reflected so many strains of American Negro thinking and feeling that it is not easy to grasp him whole. He is usually classified as a "cultural nationalist," though he was sometimes more and sometimes less. In his autobiography, *Dusk of Dawn,* published in 1940 when he was seventy-two years old, he suggested a number of different paths that American Negroes might follow, not because he thought they were necessarily the best but because white prejudice gave them no choice. He favored a path that recognized the segregation of Negroes as a fact of American life and sought to make it subject to "careful thought and intelligent planning" on the part of Negroes themselves. Instead of fighting segregation, he thought it could be used to good advantage, whatever the future might hold. Still imbued with the "double-consciousness" of his youth, he argued in favor of preparing for either eventuality—for full acceptance or full rejection by the dominant white world. Yet he warned that his path should not be mistaken "for a program of complete racial segregation and even nationalism among Negroes." The ultimate object of his "plan of action," he wrote, was "full Negro rights and Negro equality in America." But if they proved to be unattainable, he also foresaw the possibility of "eventual emigration" from the United States by "some considerable part" of the Negro population. Elsewhere in the book, he was even more pessimistic and speculated that the Negro might be "pushed out of his American fatherland" as Germany was then expelling the Jews.[2]

One side of Du Bois's thought clearly contained intellectual traces of the emigrationist tradition. He preferred to have the best of both possible worlds, but, in his most despondent moments, he felt that it might be necessary to settle for one—the African. He himself spent the last years of his life in Ghana. In his ninety-third year he officially joined the American Communist Party,[3] and a few months before his death in 1963, at the age of ninety-five, he became a citizen of Ghana. For all his vast gifts, however, Du Bois succeeded in converting few American Negroes. As he admitted, "American Negroes were not interested" in his Pan-Africanism.[4] He wanted American Negroes to lead the Negro world, but he was never able to lead American Negroes. "I never was, nor ever will be, personally popular," he wrote ruefully in his autobiography.[5] Yet by inspiring future leaders of African nationalism, such as Kwame Nkrumah and Jomo Kenyatta, he was ultimately able to influence a resurgent American black nationalism through them.

If one looks only at Dr. Du Bois's frustration in the early 1920s, one might imagine that Africa held out little appeal to the American Negroes' interests or imagination. Nothing at that very time could have been further from the truth.

In 1914 Marcus Garvey, a West Indian Negro of far more modest intellectual equipment or attainment than Dr. Du Bois, set up a Universal Negro Improvement Association in his native Jamaica. His first manifesto called on all people of

Negro or African parentage to establish "Universal Confraternity." He met with hostility or indifference. Two years later he came to New York, revived the UNIA, and, after a slow start, "stirred the imagination of the Negro masses as no Negro ever had," so James Weldon Johnson testified. And he stirred their imagination with a peculiar version of Pan-African nationalism at the very time Du Bois's Pan-Africanism could hardly get off the ground. Indeed, Garvey and Du Bois were vicious rivals and enemies. One of the least offensive things Garvey said about Du Bois was that he belonged to "the greatest enemies the black people have in the world." [6] And Du Bois, in almost the same language, paid him back: "Marcus Garvey is, without doubt, the most dangerous enemy of the Negro race in America and the world. He is either a lunatic or a traitor." [7]

Garveyism came closest to expressing itself in terms of traditional nationalism. It made "nationhood" the highest ideal of all peoples. "The Negro needs a nation and a country of his own," Garvey expounded. Or again: "Nationhood is the strongest security of any people and it is for that the Universal Negro Improvement Association strives at this time." [8] The trouble was that Garvey's proposed Negro nation was in Africa, whereas his constituency was in the United States. Garvey's "African Republic" was set up in New York, not on African soil. There was not a single African in what amounted to his African government-in-exile. This imperial travesty was headed by "His Highness, the Potentate," followed by "His Excellency, the Provisional President of Africa," and nineteen other grand dignitaries. They were surrounded by a nobility which included the Knights of the Nile, Dukes of Nigeria and Uganda, and Distinguished Service Order of Ethiopia, all in dazzling, multicolored uniforms. The military reconquest of Africa was intimated by a Universal African Legion, Universal Black Cross Nurses, Universal African Motor Corps, and Black Eagle Flying Corps. Garvey's nationalism had all the trappings and appurtenances of nationhood, except that the nation it had in mind was some-where else and had nothing to say about Garvey's plans for it.

Racism permeated Garvey's nationalism. He was obsessed with the need for "purity of race"—any race. "I believe," he said, "in a pure black race, just as how all self-respecting whites believe in a pure white race, as far as that can be." [9] The Garveyite gospel simply inverted the prejudices of white supremacy. Everything superior was black, everything inferior white. He founded an African Orthodox Church in which God was black, angels were black, and Satan was white. The church held meetings to deify the "Black Man of Sorrows" and canonize the "Black Virgin Mary."

This infatuation with racial purity was partly Garvey's un-doing. Himself black, Garvey wanted his power wholly black, to such an extent that he distinguished fundamentally not only between black and white but between black and mulatto. He tried to transplant to the United States the West Indian caste distinction between blacks and mulattoes, thereby alienating many American mulattoes. Garvey also drove the logic of "racial purity" to its most extreme by saying kind things about the Ku Klux Klan because it was openly racist as much as he was. The only whites whom he respected were those who loved Negroes as little as he loved whites. White supremacy leaders spoke at UNIA meetings, and Garvey himself once conferred with Edward Young Clarke, Imperial Giant of the Klan. Many Negroes were scandalized, but Gar-vey insisted: "I regard the Klan, the Anglo-Saxon Clubs and White American societies, as far as the Negro is concerned, as better friends of the race than all other groups of hypo-critical whites put together." [10] Garvey recognized that he and the Klan were implicitly allied, their beliefs based on a common principle—there was no place for Negroes in the United States. The only thing that mattered to him was getting the Negroes out of the United States back to where he thought they belonged—Africa. If the Ku Klux Klan helped to achieve that end by persecuting Negroes and teaching them they were not wanted, he was not against the Klan and even saw merit in it. Rarely has there been such a case of extremes meeting, or, better perhaps, feeding on each other.

Garvey's Africanism also helps to explain another paradox —his admiration for Booker T. Washington. Reading Washington's *Up from Slavery* had first inspired Garvey to become a "race leader," and thereafter he never mentioned Washington without paying tribute to his farsightedness, alone among American Negro leaders. Yet for Du Bois's generation Washington represented abject capitulation to white rule. In his famous—or infamous—address at the Atlanta Exposition in 1895, which made him the outstanding Negro spokesman for the next two decades, Washington had advised his people to strive for "material prosperity," not "social equality." "It is at the bottom of life we must begin, and not at the top," he said, and the bottom for him meant work, education, professional skills. The rest, he taught, would come in due time. Meanwhile he accepted white political domination and social ostracism. One might imagine that nothing would have been more antipathetic to Garvey's racial pride than Washington's seemingly limitless patience. On the contrary, Garvey saw in Washington an exception to other Negro movements which, Garvey complained, "sought to teach the Negro to aspire to social equality with the whites." [11]

Washington was not so much an exception to the rule as Garvey wanted to believe. Washington's doctrine of work instead of politics was a temporary expedient; he was not so much opposed to social equality and political privileges as he was convinced that they would come when the Negroes were ready for them. What Garvey read into Washington's message was the willingness to stay out of the white man's world, not to challenge him on his own ground. Garvey wanted to make a deal with white America in return for black Africa. He was ready, he said, to "cede to the white man the right of doing as he pleases in his own country, and that is why we believe in not making any trouble when he says that 'America is a white man's country,' because in the same breath and with the same determination we are going to make Africa a black man's country." [12] For Garvey, black nationalism in Africa implied white supremacy in the United States—and this equation was the reason for his peculiar affinity with both the Ku Klux Klan and Booker T. Washington.

Garveyism was also a parody of "black capitalism." The UNIA went into business on a grand scale—groceries, laundries, restaurants, hotels, printing plants, above all, the Black Star Line of ships. Logically these business enterprises should have made Garvey conscious of the fact that he was operating within the white United States economy, and not yet in his own domain where he could do as he pleased. But Garvey's business practices were also slightly fantastic. The Black Star Line's treasurer knew nothing about bookkeeping; Garvey hired and fired one executive after another on charges of dishonesty; he himself received money from stocks of which he did not bother to keep a record. It did not take long for legal and economic reality to catch up with Garvey. His movement reached its peak in 1921. In 1923 the federal government, urged by his Negro enemies, tried Garvey on a charge of using the mails to defraud in the sale of stock for his steamship line. He was convicted and sentenced to a five-year term, which he began to serve in 1925. Two years later he was pardoned and deported to Jamaica as an undesirable alien. Without him, his movement quickly shriveled. He died in London in 1940 at the age of fifty-three, broken and pathetic.[13]

In his classic work, *An American Dilemma,* Gunnar Myrdal drew the lesson that Garveyism showed that "a Negro movement in America is doomed to ultimate dissolution and collapse if it cannot gain white support." This, he continued, was the "real dilemma," for "white support will be denied to emotional Negro chauvinism when it takes organizational and political form." [14] The eminent historian John Hope Franklin concluded that Garvey's "'Negro Zionism' was doomed to failure." He tried to explain why: "Regardless of how dissatisfied Negroes were with conditions in the United States they were unwilling in the 20's, as their forebears had been a century earlier, to undertake the uncertain task of redeeming Africa. The widespread interest in Garvey's program was more a protest against the anti-Negro reaction of the postwar period than an approbation of the fantastic schemes of the Negro leader." [15] A recent writer, Harold Cruse, has expressed the view that "this predominantly West Indian movement was not really attuned to the internal peculiarities of the Negro-white situation in the United States. They saw the solution to the problem outside the system—namely, in Africa. But not a single Garveyite settlement, either in America or the West Indies, exists in Africa today." [16]

There was something both real and fantastic about Garvey's movement. That it was the first and greatest Negro mass movement in American history shows that it responded to real hopes and resentments. For all his intended appeal to Negroes everywhere, Garvey, not an American, was successful only in America and could reproduce his success nowhere else. If his flame burned more brightly than that of any other Negro leader, it was also snuffed out more quickly. For Garveyism was an authentic American Negro movement in the guise of an African fantasy. What was authentic about it made it live, however briefly; what was fantastic about it made it die out, virtually without a struggle. Despite all the propaganda about going back to Africa, no one went. Garvey himself never even visited Africa. He sent emissaries to Liberia to investigate the possibilities of colonizing it with American Negroes, but these feelers came to nothing. By 1924 relations between Garvey's movement and Liberia were so strained that Garveyites were forbidden to land in that country. Garvey appealed mainly to recently uprooted Negro migrants from the Southern states and recently arrived immigrants from the West Indies, who were stirred emotionally by an exotic incarnation of nationalism and emigrationism, even a spurious nationalism and an imaginary emigrationism. But these ideas had little or nothing to do with their immediate lives, with their own time and place. More than anything else, this was Garvey's undoing.

Self-Determination

4

Thus far we have been pursuing the first of the two predominant forms which black nationalism has traditionally assumed—external emigrationism. The other major form may be called "internal statism." It differs from the first in that it seeks to establish an independent Negro state within the confines of what is now the United States.

This scheme was also an early white idea. One of its first proponents was Anthony Benezet, a Philadelphia Huguenot, a pioneer in the antislavery movement before and after the American Revolution. In a tract called *Tyrannical Libertymen: A Discourse upon Negro Slavery in the United States,* published in Hanover, New Hampshire, in 1795, he recommended the colonization of emancipated blacks in the public lands in the Northwest Territory, then largely settled by Indians. This plan resembled the other early colonization schemes except that it envisaged a black colony on the American mainland.

Thomas Jefferson also wrestled with the problem. In a letter to James Monroe in 1801, he wondered whether it might not be advisable for the state of Virginia to purchase land north of the Ohio River for a Negro colony. He questioned, however, the desirability of establishing such a colony within the limits of the Union and bound to become part of it. His mind then turned to the possibility of locating it beyond those limits, by purchasing Indian lands on the northern frontier with British consent. Whereupon he worried that the climate would be too rigorous for black settlers. In the end he viewed the West Indies as most promising and Africa as a last resort.[1]

In Philadelphia in 1805, Thomas Brannagan published his *Serious Remonstrances Addressed to the Citizens of the Northern States and their Representatives, being an Appeal to their Natural Feelings and Common Sense; Consisting of Speculations and Animadversions, on the Recent Revival of the Slave Trade in the American Republic.* In it he made the proposal that the government should appropriate a few thousand acres of land about 2000 miles from the existing borders for the purpose of establishing a new Negro state. And in 1816 the Kentucky Abolition Society memorialized the House of Representatives in behalf of colonizing the "free people of color" on the public lands.[2] Thus, in the first two decades of the nineteenth century, colonization on the mainland and in Africa went side by side, and the latter won out only because it came to be considered more feasible.

Both whites and Negroes continued to toy with the colony or state idea for many years. A considerable number of the free black inhabitants of Richmond, Virginia, issued a statement in 1817 in support of the Colonization Society's principle of physical separation. But they wanted the black colony to be located on the Missouri River or any other place in the United States that Congress might prefer, not in

Africa.[3] In 1833 Texas was proposed as the site of a Negro colony; nothing came of it.[4] One Negro meeting in Trenton in 1831 protested against Africa but contended that "we see nothing contrary to the Constitution, to Christianity, justice, reason, or humanity, in granting us a portion of the Western territory, as a state, with the same franchise as that of Pennsylvania, New Jersey, or any other free state." Another meeting in Lewiston, Pennsylvania, the following year typically resolved "that we will not leave these United States, the land of our birth, for a home in Africa" but offered "to emigrate to any part of the United States which may be granted to us." [5]

A "Negro Exodus" took place in 1879 and 1881, mainly from Louisiana and South Carolina to Kansas. Oklahoma came in for some attention toward the end of the century. Edwin P. McCabe, a former State Auditor of Kansas, led a campaign to make Oklahoma a Negro state. An editorial in the *Indianapolis Freeman* in 1905 was convinced that "it would be an easy matter for the colored people to make Oklahoma and Indian Territory a State under their own control and management; where all the opportunities of any other American would be theirs." The editorial was probably an easy matter to write.*

The concept of a Negro state has also been one of the recurrent themes of black nationalism in the twentieth century.

---

* A deeply moving and somewhat bizarre footnote to the Oklahoma story was the career of Alfred Charles Sam, known as "Chief Sam." Claiming to be an African tribal chief born in the Gold Coast, and speaking with a British accent, he appeared in Okfuskee County in Oklahoma, where many Negroes had settled, some of them former slaves of Indians as well as of whites. How the whites shamelessly disenfranchised the Negroes in the county to gain political control is more than ever worth pondering today. To these disheartened American Negroes, "Chief Sam" came as a mysterious savior (somewhat the way "W. D. Fard" later came to the Detroit Negroes). They signed up in the hundreds, bought stock in his trading company, sold off everything they owned, and waited for him to take them to his tribal lands in the British colony. A boatload set forth in August 1914 aboard the *Liberia,* bought by Sam's company. It arrived

It was resurrected during World War I by Cyril V. Briggs, the founder of a little-known organization, the African Blood Brotherhood. Briggs, a native of the British West Indies, was an editor of the *Amsterdam News* in New York. While Garvey was coming up with his grandiose plan for a Negro state in Africa, Briggs countered with the view that the "race problem" could be solved by setting up an independent Negro nation on American territory. In editorials published in September 1917 he argued: "Considering that the more we are outnumbered, the weaker we will get, and the weaker we get the less respect, justice or opportunity we will obtain, is it not time to consider a separate political existence with a government that will represent, consider, and advance us? As one-tenth of the population, backed with many generations of unrequited toil and half a century of contribution, as free men to American prosperity, we can with reason and justice demand our portion for purposes of self-government and the pursuit of happiness, one-tenth of the territory of continental United States." He suggested locating the "colored autonomous State" in the West, either in the states of Washington, Oregon, and Idaho, or, as he thought preferable, in California and Nevada.

Briggs's anti-war stand led to his resignation from the paper. In September 1918 he began to publish a monthly magazine, the *Crusader,* which a year later became the organ of his new organization, the African Blood Brotherhood. (The name derived from an African rite of fraternization by mingling drops of blood.) It came out "for African Liberation and Redemption," which was later changed to "for immediate protection and ultimate liberation of Negroes everywhere." The first members numbered less than twenty, all

at its destination, but soon everything went wrong. Most of the emigrants eventually straggled back to the United States. The historians of this venture—a small-scale forerunner of Garveyism—comment: "They did not want to be Americans; but now they found that they did not want to be Africans either." (William E. Bittle and Gilbert Geis, *The Longest Way Home* [Detroit: Wayne State University Press, 1964], p. 196.)

in Harlem and most of them West Indian in origin. The organization spread to other parts of the United States and the West Indies but never exceeded 3000 members even at its peak. Set up as a secret revolutionary organization, little was known of it for a long time. Whereas Briggs had demanded a state within the United States in the *Amsterdam News*, he changed his mind in the *Crusader*. In 1919 he came out for a Negro state in Africa, South America, or the Caribbean, to which American Negroes could emigrate. Gradually he linked the national and social elements in his thinking, as in this prescription in 1921: "The surest and quickest way, then, in our opinion, to achieve the salvation of the Negro is to combine the two most likely and feasible propositions, viz.: salvation for all Negroes through the establishment of a strong, stable, independent Negro State (along the lines of our own race genius) in Africa and elsewhere; and salvation for all Negroes (as well as other oppressed people) through the establishment of a Universal Socialist Co-operative commonwealth." [6]

In effect, Briggs wanted a Negro state, and it was not so important where. Though he and Garvey were both West Indians and their aims were not fundamentally dissimilar, they staged one of the most bitter internecine battles of the period. Briggs criticized Garvey for running a one-man movement. When Garvey rejected an offer of cooperation, Briggs accused him of "loose chatter and mock heroics." Garvey hit back at the light-complexioned Briggs by calling him a white man passing himself off as a Negro—a favorite Garveyite anathema. Briggs sued for libel, and Garvey was forced to apologize publicly.[7]

This mix-up shows how complex were the personal and political factors in the pro-African movements. In these very years, Garvey, Du Bois, and Briggs were working toward some form of the same end. Garvey was ostensibly all Back-to-Africa, but his only mass constituency was in, and never moved from, the United States. Du Bois was interested in working for Africa from a base in the United States. Briggs started out by locating his Negro state in the United States rather than in Africa, but the lure of Africa proved too strong for him too, and he gave his organization an African name, besides conceding that Africa might be more suitable than the United States. Africa beckoned to all of them, and it was just as far away as it had been for a century.

Briggs and the African Blood Brotherhood have a special interest because they provided, in 1921, the first Negro contingent for the American Communist movement, which had been founded two years earlier. Besides Briggs, Richard B. Moore, Lovett Fort-Whiteman, Otto Hall and his brother Haywood Hall (better known as Harry Haywood) were recruited into the party from the Brotherhood. Otto Hall's political itinerary was symptomatic of the times. He had served overseas in the United States Army in World War I, and, having been told that he had been "fighting for democracy," upon his return he became discontented and disillusioned with the democracy he found for his own people at home. He attended one of Garvey's spectacular meetings in Chicago, was swept into the UNIA, and signed up as an officer in the "Black Legion." When a friend gave him a copy of Briggs's new magazine, the *Crusader,* he liked its more "social" appeal even better and joined the first post of the African Blood Brotherhood organized in Chicago in 1919. Two years later he followed Briggs into the Communist movement.[8] In this way they moved far to the "Left" of Garvey, who frowned on both Communism and trade unionism as white movements. Garvey once denounced white Communists and trade unionists as "more dangerous to the Negro's welfare than any other group at present." He was, in fact, a devotee of capitalism; those who "unreasonably and wantonly oppose or fight against it," he said, "are enemies to human advancement."[9] Those who today identify themselves with one side of Garveyism might do well to look at some of the other sides.

Insofar as it was Africa-oriented, the African Blood Brother-hood was another fantasy-infected movement. That its leaders could go over to Communism, which then strongly opposed any kind of African orientation for American Negroes, showed how superficial the Brotherhood's Africanism had been. It was one more indication that Negroes were looking for something they could not find in America, but it did not prove that they could find it in Africa.

The second and more important Negro state theory was advanced by the Communists at the end of the 1920s. Before that, the Communists had carried on the older American radical tradition based on racial equality. At its third con-vention at the end of 1923, for example, the American party had repudiated the Back-to-Africa movement as "only an evasion of the real struggle and an excuse to surrender the Negroes' rights in their native land, America." It called the United States "the home of the American Negro" and championed "his full, free, and equal partnership with his white brothers in the future society."

The idea that the Negroes in the United States constituted a "national question" seems to have originated with Joseph Stalin, who first mentioned it in 1925 to Otto Hall, one of five Negroes who went to Moscow to study at the Communist University of Toilers of the East, which specialized in two groups of students—one from the Soviet East and the other from colonial and dependent countries. No one paid much attention to Stalin's suggestion until the doctrine of "the right of self-determination of the Negroes in the Black Belt" was adopted in a preliminary form at the Sixth World Con-gress of the Communist International in the summer of 1928. It was revised and issued in final form two years later.

At that time, 72.6 per cent of all Negroes in the United States still lived in twelve Southern states, and 51.1 per cent in the rural portions of those states. In 189 counties of this area, Negroes accounted for more than half the population.

The "Black Belt" was defined as that area in which there was a substantial Negro majority, plus a larger area of 477 counties in which Negroes constituted 44.8 per cent of the total population. Thus a map could be—and was—drawn of the Black Belt and the so-called Border Territory, where the Negroes were supposedly entitled to "the right to self-determination." [10]

This theory distinguished sharply between the North and the South. It recognized that the Negro masses in the North were "working for assimilation." Therefore it made "equal rights" the main slogan in the North and a subordinate one in the South. If Negroes wanted their own special schools or "government organs," Communists were told to support them, but such demands were expected primarily in the South, not the North. In the Communist Party and its "auxiliary" fronts, however, Negro segregation was ruled out; they were required to bring blacks and whites together more closely than before.

Thus the Communist program tried to establish a delicate balance between black-and-white integration (or "assimilation," as it used to be called) and black nationalism. Even the latter was also very delicately equilibrated. The *right* to Negro self-determination in the Black Belt was stressed, but not necessarily its *realization*. At one point, early in 1930, the American Communists interpreted the policy to mean the right of self-determination "to the point of separation." But the then acting secretary went to Moscow for consultations and was told, on the highest authority—no doubt Stalin himself—that this phrase went too far and had to be deleted.[11] The final version left open whether the Negroes themselves would want to set up an independent Negro state. "Complete right to self-determination includes also the right to governmental separation, but does not necessarily imply that the Negro population should *make use of this* right in all circumstances, that is, that it must actually separate or attempt to separate the Black Belt from the

existing governmental federation with the United States,"
it stated. "If it desires to separate, it must be free to do so;
but if it prefers to remain federated with the United States
it must also be free to do that" (italics in original). If and
when a "proletarian revolution" took place in the United
States, moreover, Negro Communists were advised to come
out against complete separation from the United States and
to try to convince the Negro population in the Black Belt
that federation was more desirable.[12]

This position may be described as conditional Negro
statism. The Communists held on to it militantly for about
five years, until the Popular Front policy was adopted in
1935. As they later admitted, it fell on deaf ears and drew almost no support outside the party itself, going much too far
for most Negroes and not far enough for the extreme nationalists. If the Communists made any progress among Negroes
in the 1930s, it was due to their militant championing of
"equal rights," not "self-determination." One reason for the
failure of self-determination was that it went against the tide
of history. While the Communists were discovering the Black
Belt, it was already breaking up. About 200,000 Negroes
migrated north annually after 1916.* This exodus was
slowed during the depression, but it picked up momentum
toward the end of the 1930s and turned into a flood in the
next two decades. By 1960 Negroes in the twelve Southern
states accounted for only 53.5 per cent of the total Negro
population and those in the rural portions only 23.7 per cent
of the total population. In effect, the Black Belt has been
getting smaller and less black for half a century, gradually
cutting the ground from under the thesis of its "self-determination."

The American Communists were not the only ones who

---

* The number of counties in the twelve Southern states in which Negroes comprised half or more of the population went down from 262 in
1910 to 222 in 1920, 190 in 1930, 178 in 1940, 151 in 1950, and 134 in
1960.

flirted with some form of "self-determination" in the 1930s. A Chicago lawyer, Oscar C. Brown, tried to set up a non-Communist movement "for the establishment of the Forty-Ninth State," which he envisaged as "not a separate nation but an interdependent commonwealth like any other of the present forty-eight states." It was launched in the mid-30s, just as the Communists were beginning to soft-pedal their program for the Black Belt, and Brown was no more successful. The Forty-Ninth State idea never caught on.

Curiously, the most tenacious advocate of Negro "self-determination" in that decade was Leon Trotsky. In 1933 he advised his reluctant American followers to support the Negroes' right "to separate a piece of land for themselves," whether or not they were a majority in any state, and he held out the possibility that the Negroes might well get to the "proletarian dictatorship" ahead of the white workers through the medium of self-determination. Again in 1939 he insisted that the American Trotskyists should take a positive position with respect to a demand for self-determination, as long as it came from the Negroes themselves. "If you wish to take part of the country, it is all right," he told his American disciples to say, "but we do not wish to make the decision for you." [13]

In 1946 the official American Communists decided to revive and then again in 1959 to withdraw the old line that the Negro problem was "national" in character. But in 1968 one old-time Negro Communist, Claude Lightfoot, tried to resurrect the old line in a revised version. In order to meet the objection that the black majority no longer lived in the Black Belt, he put forward the idea that self-determination should apply "to the people as a whole and not to a territorial unity." Other Negro Communist leaders were not convinced.[14] The Communists have been extraordinarily unlucky in their position on self-determination. When they came out for it in the early 1930s the American Negroes were not interested. No sooner had they formally withdrawn it than black nationalism began to revive. They might even give it the kiss of death, if Lightfoot should have his way, by coming out for it again.

Thus the internal-state form of black nationalism in America has had almost as long and varied a career as its chief rival, the emigrationist form. This bifurcation is not usual in nationalist movements and suggests a combination of needs which neither one could satisfy by itself.

Emigrationism satisfied the fundamentally negative need at the core of black nationalism in America—the need to renounce a country in which enslavement prevailed at worst and inequality persisted at best. But the positive need—to adopt another country—was more difficult to satisfy. Emigrationism forced black Americans to identify themselves nationally with either an existing black state, such as Liberia or Haiti, or with a blackness that was more a state of mind than a nation-state. The identification with any particular black state was never possible for enough black Americans because they did not come from any of them and because these states were too far removed socially and culturally to be preferable to even an inferior status in the United States. The alternative has been to conceive of a more amorphous, generalized black nationalism that would take in all black peoples everywhere. The trouble with stretching the term too far is that it takes in too much to be an effective nationalism. In the white world, there are French nationalism, German nationalism, Irish nationalism, and the like, but there is no such thing as "white nationalism." "White," "black," "brown," and "yellow" refer to something much larger and more inclusive than nationalism, which by its very nature at this stage divides blacks from blacks as well as whites from whites. For a black American to emigrate has been a way of evading the problem of black nationalism in America, not of meeting it.

From this point of view, a black state within the confines

of the present United States would more nearly represent a genuinely American black nationalism. It would confer nationhood on black Americans themselves and not make them an appendage of some other black nation far away. Yet, historically, a strictly American black nationalism has been so difficult to envision, to locate, to make economically viable, that it has never succeeded in becoming a movement anywhere as large as that led by Bishop Turner or Marcus Garvey. The reason would seem to be that emigrationism has had, at least superficially, a quick and easy recipe—back to Africa or on to Haiti—even if it is easier said than done. Internal statism poses such formidable conceptual problems that none of its proponents ever succeeded in coping with them seriously. The Communists at least started with what seemed to them solid ground—a black majority in a determinate territory. Apart from everything else, the ground refused to remain firm. Those who, as we shall see, took up the same idea in the nineteen-sixties might have done well to heed that lesson.

The Nation of Islam

5

We have now come to the forms which black nationalism in America is taking at the present time. The oldest and largest contemporary black nationalist movement is the Nation of Islam, better known as the Black Muslims.

The legendary origins of this movement come close to pure fantasy. It seems to have its roots in the first "Back-to-Islam" movement, founded by a native of North Carolina, Timothy Drew, who changed his name to Noble Drew Ali.* From his picture he appeared to be a tall, slender, dark Negro, with the aspect of a

---

* The attraction of Islam for Western Negroes goes even further back. One of the forerunners of present-day black nationalism, Edward W. Blyden, wrote an essay praising Islamism at the expense of Christianity for African Negroes as early as 1875 (*Christianity, Islam and the Negro Race* [London: W. B. Whittingham, 1888], pp. 1–29). Blyden was born in the West Indies, came to the United States in 1850, and later settled in Liberia, where he engaged in *Christian* missionary work.

"dreamer," dressed in dark trousers, dark shoes, a white robe and sash, collar and necktie, topped with a fez. He began by speaking to small groups of Negroes on street corners and in basements or empty lots. In 1913 or thereabouts, at the age of twenty-seven, he is reputed to have set up a "Moorish-American Science Temple" in Newark, New Jersey, where he is said to have worked as an expressman. In the next decade and a half, other temples were opened in Pittsburgh, Detroit, Chicago, and elsewhere. Thus Garvey's Back-to-Africa-ism and Drew Ali's Back-to-Islamism flourished at about the same time, though the former at its height reached many more people than the latter.

With little formal education, Drew Ali hit on the idea that American Negroes could achieve salvation simply by making themselves into "Asiatics" or, more specifically, into Moors or Moorish-Americans whose ancestors had come from Morocco. He also taught that these Moorish-Americans were descendants of the ancient Moabites who had inhabited the northwestern and southwestern shores of Africa—not, as formerly believed, the region east of the Dead Sea. He gave membership cards to those who joined his cult, certifying that they were Moslems "under the Divine Laws of the Holy Koran of Mecca." He composed a 64-page *Holy Koran*—only the title was the same as the sacred book of the Islamic religion—which his devotees were enjoined to guard as a secret. It proclaimed that Noble Drew Ali was a prophet ordained by Allah, akin to Confucius, Jesus, Buddha, and Zoroaster. Subordinate leaders were generally known as "Sheiks." For Drew Ali a change of name was apparently thaumaturgic. White Europeans had subjugated the Moorish-Americans—whose color he taught was olive, not black—by calling them Negroes, colored, black, or Ethiopian. By casting off these names in favor of "Moorish-Americans," they could regain their true identity and freedom. Thus Drew Ali provided American Negroes with a new national origin that made them part of a far-flung Moorish Nation that had somehow made its way to North America.

This new nationality was the key to Drew Ali's teachings and influence. "Before you can have a God," he preached, "you must have a nationality." He invoked Garvey's name by suggesting that Garvey was to him as John the Baptist was to Christ. Unlike Garvey, however, he did not tell his followers to leave the United States or to found an independent state. When the Garvey movement ran into trouble in the mid-20s, Drew Ali warned all his "Moors" to "cease from all radical or agitating speeches" and to leave the "Europeans" alone in order not to cause "confusion." In effect, Drew Ali's emigrationism was purely psychological. It was enough for American Negroes to identify with an Islamic African nation and adopt its religion, if only in name. Thereafter they merely had to wait for the inevitable destruction of white or European rule, of which the sign from heaven would be a star within a crescent moon. Meanwhile they could be loyal citizens of the United States and pledge allegiance to its flag. Drew Ali was also something of a practical man for all his dreamy appearance; one of his sidelines was a profitable business that sold Old Moorish Healing Oil, Moorish Purifier Bath Compound, and Moorish Herb Tea for Human Ailments.

Chicago became Drew Ali's main stronghold. As Garveyism declined, Drew Ali's movement grew large enough to be worth fighting over. In 1929 Drew Ali's supreme leadership was challenged by Sheik Claude Greene, allegedly a small-time politician and former butler of the philanthropist Julius Rosenwald. In the struggle between their factions, Greene was shot and stabbed to death in March 1929. Drew Ali was arrested and charged with the killing. Released on bond, he died a few weeks later, mysteriously. His followers soon split among themselves, each strong man with his own temple.[1]

"Moorish Science" was not the only form of psychological emigrationism. As early as 1900, it is said, Negro preachers traveled through the Carolinas spreading the word that the so-called American Negroes were really the lost sheep of Israel. About 1915, at the same time Drew Ali's cult was coming up, the first "Black Jewish" or "Black Hebrew" congregation was organized by F. S. Cherry, an amiable, dark brown ex-seaman and ex-railway employee. He was born somewhere in the deep South and claimed that once in his travels, far from his native land, the Lord had approached him in a vision and had touched him. Thus appointed a Prophet, he was led back to America and directed to establish the Church of God, as it was officially known, in Philadelphia. Also self-educated, he picked up some Yiddish and Hebrew, and impressed his followers by quoting from the Talmud as well as from the Bible. The Lord also thoughtfully gave Prophet Cherry the exclusive right to profanity, which he liked to use.[2]

The largest sect of "Black Jews," numbering about 1000, is now in Harlem. According to Howard Brotz, who has studied them, they believe that they really derive from the Ethiopian Hebrews, or Falashas, and that slavery robbed them of their true identity.[3] Otherwise they are as little related to the traditional Jews in their beliefs and services as the Black Muslims are to the traditional Mohammedans. The important thing seems to be, in both cases, a new national origin, neither American nor African, neither white nor Christian. Psychological emigrationism of the Moorish Science or Black Jewish type makes it possible to reject the status of being an American Negro without accepting a pro-white orientation. In the case of the Black Jews, this is achieved by identifying with the Biblical patriarchs, who were allegedly black. Its substitute nationalism assumes a purely spiritual or religious form, about which nothing more needs to be done because Allah or the Messiah will take care of its fulfillment in His own good time. Most likely, however, it serves much the same purpose as a more mundane nationalism.*

In any case, the "Islamic" line of black nationalism did not die out with Drew Ali.

In July 1930 a stranger suddenly appeared in Detroit. His name was usually given as Wallace D. or W. D. Fard. One of his first converts related: "He came first to our houses selling raincoats, and afterwards silks. In this way he could get into the people's houses, for every woman was eager to see the nice things the peddlers had for sale." Then he dropped a hint of something more to come: "He told us that the silks he carried were the same kind that our people used in their home country and that he had come from there. So we all asked him to tell us about our own country."

The mysterious stranger suggested a meeting in someone's house to hear his story. One of his first listeners recalled that he said: "My name is W. D. Fard and I came from the Holy City of Mecca. More about myself I will not tell you yet, for the time has not yet come. I am your brother. You have not yet seen me in my royal robes." His "light color" and "oriental" features fostered the belief that he was a Moslem. One story had him born in Mecca, the son of a wealthy member of the very tribe to which the Prophet Mohammed had himself belonged. Another tale gave him a British education in preparation for a career in the diplomatic service of the Kingdom of Hejaz.

Soon Fard came to be regarded as a prophet in his own right, sent to bring freedom, justice, and equality to his black brethren in North America, who, he said, belonged to the same race as his own. He spoke in mysterious metaphors

* In 1967, 186 "Black Jews" emigrated to Gbatala, Liberia, of whom 86 were left in 1969. They were led by Ben Ammi, formerly Ben Carter of Chicago, and hoped to make their way to Israel (*Amsterdam News*, October 18, 1969, p. 4). Thirty-nine emigrated to Israel at the end of 1969 (*The New York Times*, December 23, 1969).

—of the Black Nation as his "Uncle" and its white oppressor as the "Cave Man," "Satan," and the "blue-eyed devils." He slowly weaned his followers away from the Bible to the Koran, as the violence of his anti-white teachings increased. His esoteric doctrine was set forth in one written text, *Teaching for the Lost Found Nation of Islam in a Mathematical Way*, and an orally transmitted text in two parts, *Secret Ritual of the Nation of Islam*.

A University of Michigan sociologist who saw these texts in the late 1930s summed up their message as follows:

> The black men in North America are not Negroes, but members of the lost tribe of Shabazz, stolen by traders from the Holy City of Mecca 379 years ago. The prophet came to America to find and to bring back to life his long lost brethren, from whom the Caucasians had taken away their language, their nation and their religion. Here in America they were living other than themselves. They must learn that they are the original people, noblest of the nations of the earth. The Caucasians are the colored people, since they have lost their original color. The original people must regain their religion, which is Islam, their language, which is Arabic, and their culture, which is astronomy and higher mathematics, especially calculus. They must live according to the law of Allah, avoiding all meat of "poison animals," hogs, ducks, geese, 'possums and catfish. They must give up completely the use of stimulants, especially liquor. They must clean themselves up—both their bodies and their houses. If in this way they obeyed Allah, he would take them back to the Paradise, from which they had been stolen —The Holy City of Mecca.[4]

It could not have been easy for most of Fard's followers to understand much of what he said. Almost all of them were poor, illiterate migrants from the most rural districts of the southern states. Some had dimly heard of Garvey and Noble Drew Ali, both of whom agreed that their homeland was in Africa or in Morocco but at least not in the United States. As C. Eric Lincoln, one of the main students of the Black

Muslim movement, notes, Fard helped his follower to relive, "at least in fantasy, the glorious history of Black Afro-Asia." [5]

The first Temple of Islam was organized in Detroit. It grew rapidly and gave rise to subsidiary organizations. A "University of Islam" professed to teach "knowledge of our own," ostensibly Moslem, rather than "the civilization of the Caucasian devils." A Moslem Girls' Training and General Civilization Class taught women how to clean and cook. A military group, known as the "Fruit of Islam," was set up to give male members instruction in weapons and tactics. When the job of running the entire movement proved to be too much for Fard, he appointed a Minister of Islam to take charge and a staff of assistant ministers responsible to the Minister. The police began to pay attention to him, owing to rumors of "blood sacrifice" in his cult, and Fard was jailed in 1932. He was ordered out of Detroit on May 26, 1933, moved to Chicago that same year, and was almost immediately arrested there.[6] Perhaps for this reason, Fard withdrew more and more from public view. As his followers saw less and less of him, they came to believe that he was indeed, as he was reputed to have told the Detroit police, "the Supreme Ruler of the Universe," or, as he was now calling himself, "God Allah."

Politically, Fard's doctrine was clearly nationalistic. His message was addressed to a nation—the "Nation of Islam." Those who belonged to this nation were not Americans and were to have as little as possible to do with American institutions. They were citizens of the Holy City of Mecca, not American citizens. Their flag was the Moslem flag, not the American flag. Their children belonged in the University of Islam, not in American schools. They were not obliged to obey the American Constitution or serve in American armed forces. One splinter group refused to go along with Fard's anti-Americanism and made loyalty to the American Constitution and the American flag their cardinal principle. The split showed that Fard's earliest followers were not unmindful of the effect of his nationalism on their status as Americans.

In late 1933 or some time in 1934 Fard disappeared as suddenly and mysteriously as he had appeared. His followers apparently divided into two camps—those who recognized his divinity as Allah, the true God, and those who did not. The former, known as the "Temple People," accepted as their leader one of Fard's chief lieutenants, Elijah Poole.

According to his own story, Poole was born in 1898 in Georgia, the son of a rural Negro preacher. He says that he attended public school in Georgia, but the author of the foreword to his book was permitted to make known that "he learned only the bare rudiments of reading, writing, and arithmetic before he had to go to the fields to help his family earn a living." [7] In his early twenties, he worked in Macon, Georgia, for the Southern Railway Company and the Cherokee Brick Company, at the latter as a tramroad foreman and builder. He married and had two children before moving to Detroit in April 1923 at the age of twenty-five. He first met W. D. Fard in 1931, the year after the latter's arrival in Detroit. As Poole rose in the movement, Fard first renamed him "Karriem" and then "Muhammad." He appointed Elijah Muhammad his chief Minister of Islam, and the latter also moved to Chicago, which he made his permanent base of operations. After Fard disappeared, Elijah Muhammad began to teach that Mr. W. F. Muhammad or Master W. Fard Muhammad or Master Fard Muhammad, as he called him at different times, had been none other than Allah, God in person, the long-awaited Messiah of the Christians and the Mahdi of the Moslems. With Fard elevated to the status of Allah, Elijah Muhammad took over as His Prophet or as the "Messenger of Allah."

Once upon a time there was a boy named Yakub. He was born 6600 years ago, twenty miles from the present Holy

City of Mecca. When he was six years old he said: "Uncle, when I get to be an old man, I am going to make a people who shall rule you." The Uncle said: "What will you make; something to make mischief and cause bloodshed in the land?" Yakub answered: "Nevertheless, Uncle, I know that which you do not know."

The uncle was the Black Nation which then covered the entire world. Yakub was a god of the Black Nation. Because his head was so large, they used to call him the "big-head scientist." Everyone was and would still be black if it were not for Yakub. After graduating at the age of eighteen from all the colleges and universities of the Black Nation, he discovered that the black man had two germs in him—one black, the other brown. He realized that he could graft these germs in such a way that, finally, he could make a white man. He wanted these white men to rule over the Black Nation for a long time. He promised a luxurious life to those who would follow him. He became so dangerous that the King decided to send him and 59,999 of his followers into exile on the island of Pelan or Patmos in the Aegean Sea.

There Yakub carried out his devilish experiments. He killed all the black babies by pricking their brains with a sharp needle and saved only the brown ones. It took him two hundred years to make all the babies brown, then another two hundred years to make them all yellow or red, and still another two hundred years to produce an all-pale white race on this island. Adam was the name of the first white man. Mr. Yakub lived only a hundred and fifty years, but his assistants carried on after him. Thus Yakub succeeded in making devils which were pale white with blue eyes, the ugliest colors, as everyone knows, and he called them "Caucasians." When these white devils returned to the Holy Land of Islam, they set the people of the Black Nation against each other. In six months civil war broke out. The holy men went to the King and asked his advice. The King told them that all the trouble was caused by the white devils.

So the King decided to drive the white devils out of his land, out of Paradise, across the hot, sandy desert to the west, to what is now called Europe. They lived in hills and caves as savages for the next two thousand years. Then Musa (Moses) was born, four thousand years ago, and Allah sent him to the exiled devils in Europe to civilize them. Moses had such a hard time that he once blew up about three hundred of the worst troublemakers with a few sticks of dynamite. When the imams or scientists protested, Moses said: "If you only knew how much trouble these devils give me, you would do as I do." After Moses came Jesus, two thousand years ago, who also gave up in his effort to convert the Jews or white race to the religion of Islam. After Jesus came Muhammad, fifteen hundred years ago, and he was so troubled by the impossibility of reforming the white devils that he suffered a heart attack and died at the age of sixty-two and a half.

This is how Europe was populated with white devils. Nevertheless, they owed their existence to the original race of black men, from whom they came and to whom they must return. The white devils were created to be the enemy of black mankind for six thousand years. This period expired in 1914, because World War I marked the fall of white power. The final conflict between Allah and the white devils draws dangerously close. The end of white rule may even come in a matter of minutes. Of all the white countries, Allah wishes to destroy America and its people first. Already in 1931, God, in the person of Fard Muhammad, informed his Messenger, Elijah Muhammad, that America was No. 1 on his list of enemies doomed to destruction, that America and Germany were the "two worst vicious, evil destructive troublemakers of the entire nation earth." The fall of America will be like the fall of ancient Babylon. In less than forty years there may not be a white man in the Western hemisphere. After the white man goes, there will never again be a trouble-making people on our planet. After the present world is destroyed, the righteous will come into their own, with no end of peace, joy, and happiness.

Who are the so-called Negroes who now live in America, and what does the future hold for them? They are descendants of the original Black Nation of Asia, of the Great Asiatic Nation, of the Asiatic Nation from the continent of Africa. Specifically, they belong to the tribe of Shabazz, which was originally the tribe that came with this part of the earth sixty trillion years ago when a great explosion divided the earth from the moon. The tribe of Shabazz first discovered which part of this planet was best to inhabit—the rich Nile Valley of Egypt and the Holy City of Mecca in Arabia. And fifty thousand years ago one of the tribe's dissatisfied scientists wanted to make the tribe tough and hard in order to endure the jungles and to overcome the beasts in Africa, which is East Asia. But he failed to get others to agree with him, with the result that he produced a people with kinky hair. This people was lost from the tribe of Shabazz for four hundred years and delivered into slavery. Within the larger Black Nation, the so-called Negroes brought to America make up the Nation of Islam which constitutes a chosen people, appointed to lead the way toward destruction of the present dominant white civilization. Master Fard and then His Prophet, Elijah Muhammad, were sent to find them and to bring them back to the Black Nation from which they had come. For this reason, they are "lost-found members of the Asiatic Nation." Allah prophesied that the four hundred years of slavery would end in 1955, and the time has now come for Allah to give His people their own home.

For those who accept Allah and Islam, there will be a hereafter, but it will be on earth, not in the sky, and for flesh and blood, not for "spooks." Elijah Muhammad has promised: "It will be the heaven of the righteous forever! No sickness, no hospitals, no insane asylums, no gambling, no cursing, or swearing will be seen or heard in that life." And he added: "You will be clothed in silk interwoven with gold and eat the best of food that you desire."

All this and more, Master Fard Muhammad, who was none other than Allah in person, revealed to his Prophet and Messenger, Elijah Muhammad, in Detroit between 1931 and 1933. *As-Salaam-Aliakum.*[8]

This mythology obviously contains a potentially explosive mixture. If it has not erupted more forcefully, the cause partly lies in the eschatology itself. Inasmuch as Allah has already decreed the total, apocalyptic victory of the Black Nation, the "so-called Negroes" of America—as Elijah Muhammad always calls them—can afford to wait for the promised day of judgment in the United States. With Allah on their side, "you don't need Navys, ground forces, air forces, standing armies to fight this last war," he has assured them. Thus, in Black Muslim doctrine, violence can be forsworn and faith can be put wholly in self-help and self-awareness. In this way, Elijah Muhammad's practical politics have tended to reduce rather than to exacerbate black-white confrontations.

Curiously, however, his black nationalism is not quite consistent with his cosmology. The latter implies that the so-called Negroes or Nation of Islam need wait only a little while longer to inherit the white man's world. Yet, as a practical matter, Elijah Muhammad protests against waiting and would be satisfied with only part of the whole now.

In almost the same words as those of Martin Delany over a hundred years ago, Elijah Muhammad has exclaimed: "We are a Nation in a nation." That he means a traditional, conventional nation is clear: "We want to build a nation that will be recognized as a nation, that will be self-respecting and receive respect of the other nations of the earth." He also recognizes land as the key to nationhood: "We must understand the importance of land to our nation. The first and most important reason that the individual countries of Europe, Africa and Asia are recognized as nations is because they occupy a specific area of the earth." [9]

But where is the land? Here he is not so sure and, in fact, gives seemingly contradictory answers. Sometimes he appears to imply that the so-called Negroes should not stay in the United States and should go back where they came from—in the East. On one occasion he said: "Let us go back to our native land and people. Every Muslim can go." And again: "America is falling; she is a habitation of devils and every uncleanness and hateful people of the righteous. Forsake her and fly to your own before it is too late." But, in two of his most explicit statements on the subject, he paradoxically gave the whites the option to decide where the new nation might be. In a 10-Point Program and Position, entitled "What Do the Muslims Want," Point 4 reads:

> 4. We want our people in America whose parents or grandparents were descendants from slaves to be allowed, to establish a separate state or territory of their own—either on this continent or elsewhere. We believe that our former slave-masters are obligated to provide such land and that the area must be fertile and minerally rich. We believe that our former slave-masters are obligated to maintain and supply our needs in this separate territory for the next twenty or twenty-five years until we are able to produce and supply our own needs.

And to a question from the *New York Herald Tribune* he replied:

> The American white man is not going to move out of his estate to give to the so-called Negroes. We are not asking you to do any such thing.
> No, only unless you prevent our going to our own. If you are going to prevent us from going to our own, or back where we came from, where you found us, then give us a place here to ourselves.
> There has been too much talk about separation and

about our acting or demanding a territory here. We're not demanding territory in America. No, sir, we're asking America only if they don't allow us to go back to our own people and to the country from which we came.

Then give us a place to ourselves; as you know and we have learned through experience for 400 years, we can't get along in peace together. You're not going to accept us as your equals, and we know you're not going to do so. We disregard your promises because you are not going to live up to them; because 100 per cent of your people will not agree with such. And we have proof today in the South.[10]

In 1959, however, Muhammad clearly demanded territory in America. In a speech at Washington, D.C., he declared:

Give us three, four, or more states. We have well earned whatever they give us; they give us twenty-five states, we have well earned them. Give us a territory. Give us the same instrument that they had to start a civilization in that territory. Take care of us. Give us what we ask them for, for the next twenty-five years until we are able to go for ourselves. Demand something. Don't demand a job. Demand some earth. We have come to the point we must have a home on this earth that we can call our own.

Later in the same speech he added: "They will never give us three or four states. That I probably know, but that doesn't hinder you and me from asking for it." [11]

In 1966, Muhammad's followers bought an 1800-acre farm in Dawson, Georgia, which they were able to operate peacefully and successfully. In 1969, however, when they purchased two farms of 376 and 541 acres in St. Clair County, Alabama, the local white residents rose angrily in protest and made strenuous efforts to oust them, including threats of violence. Though the Muslims protested that they merely sought to raise crops and cattle for their restaurants and supermarkets in Chicago and elsewhere, many whites raised the specter of a Muslim take-over of the Southern states by training people "to start their new nation here." There might have been trouble in this rural Alabama area anyway, but the little-understood Muslim program of black nationhood enabled the white opposition to season their social discrimination with unwonted patriotic fervor.[12]

Thus Muhammad has called for going back to a "native land," which, according to his cosmology, could only be somewhere in Asia or Africa; for a separate state either on the American continent or elsewhere; and for three, four, or more states of the present United States. He has also maintained that all the white people in the Western Hemisphere really belong in Europe, which was given to the whites, according to the cosmology. This has led to the idea that one way of handling the problem would be for all whites to return to Europe instead of sending all blacks back to Africa.[13] For the time being, however, Muhammad has indicated that he would agree to settle for less. Point 7 of his Program and Position says: "As long as we are not allowed to establish a state or territory of our own, we demand not only equal justice under the laws of the United States but equal employment opportunities—NOW!" Other points demand equal education and prohibition of intermarriage.[14] On occasion Muhammad has even forgotten his own contempt and antipathy for the whites and has told his people to learn from them. In an "economic blueprint," Point 5 reads: "Observe the operations of the white man. He is successful. He makes no excuses for his failures. He works hard in a collective manner. You do the same." [15]

That the Nation of Islam represents some form of black nationalism is unmistakable. But it is not so clear what and where the Black Nation is. Yet, if its black nationalism cannot take a positive form, it can at least be negative. The Muslims may not know where their own land, their own nation, is now, but they can renounce the American state and nation. Muhammad teaches that "we (so-called Negroes) are not and cannot be American citizens, since we are not

American by nature or race." [16] On one point he has always been adamant and consistent—the separation of whites and blacks. Whether here or there, he has insisted that "this is the time in history for the separation of the so-called Negroes and the so-called white Americans." [17] This separation can take a psychological, a religious, and an economic form even if it cannot express itself in the ultimate guise of a national territory. In this respect, Muhammad's activities resemble those of Marcus Garvey, for whom Muhammad has understandably expressed "a very high opinion." Like the Garveyites, the Muslims believe in a completely separate black economy and have also set up numerous communal businesses, including farms, groceries, restaurants, and clothing stores. In their economic emphasis, the Muslims also go back to the tradition of Booker T. Washington, without his adaptive political overtones.

In its internal structure, the Nation of Islam is built on strictly authoritarian state-within-a-state lines. Elijah Muhammad, the Messenger, is the latter-day equivalent of an all-powerful theocratic ruler. He heads, by divine right, with absolute authority, the counterpart of a church-state. Under him, subject to his supreme will, are the Ministers of each Temple, whom he alone appoints; the Supreme Captains in charge of various subsidiary organizations, also responsible only to him; and a hierarchy of lower officers: captains; first, second, and third lieutenants; investigators; secretaries. The Muslims have the rudiments of an independent economy, a school system, a self-defense corps, vocational training, and even their own flag. Of the Fruit of Islam, the self-defense corps, E. U. Essien-Udom has remarked: "Ideologically, the organization fits into the general belief of the Muslims that the Nation of Islam is a nation within a nation, and as such must have its own government." [18]

The Black Muslims show how many different elements and influences can go into a single case-history of black nationalism—ethnological fantasy, theological credulity, internal statism, psychological emigrationism, economic separatism, political isolationism, and individual self-improvement. If they cannot have a nation, they can have separatist substitutes for a nation, promissory notes of sovereignty, symbolic globules of self-determination. That they cannot have the real thing suggests how limited and unsatisfactory this manifestation of black nationalism may be for the vast majority of American Negroes who cannot lose themselves in the Muslim fantasy-world.* But for those who can and do, it must answer a real need. Thus far the movement has mainly attracted the poorest and least-educated Negroes in the North, many of them born in the South. From all accounts, it has given them new dignity, self-discipline, and social responsibility. Whatever fantasy there may be in its black nationalism, the Nation of Islam provides a new day-by-day reality for those whom Elijah Muhammad once called "Negroes in the mud," and thus, paradoxically, enables them to live more happily and productively in the here and now. The political and theological mystique may be a small price to pay for the simple, homely virtues inculcated by the Messenger of Allah, who also wages a holy war against drunkenness, delinquency, drug addiction, prostitution, idleness, ignorance, and self-denigration.

* Yet it is curious that the Muslims, adherents of Islam, should have been chosen to play this role. The Arabs were among the great slave traders in Africa from the earliest times. One authority writes: "Negroes were being shipped across the Red Sea and the Indian Ocean at least from the first century A.D. The trade was never interrupted until recent times, and though the market was not as insatiable as that created by the West in America, the total toll of Arabia and Asia over a period of 1,800 years may well have been greater than the formidable millions quoted for the Atlantic trade." (F. George Kay, *The Shameful Trade* [London: Frederick Muller, 1967], p. 180.)

Malcolm X

6

And so black nationalism continues to haunt American Negro movements and messiahs. It has just enough reality to recur in new manifestations and just enough unreality to revive old fantasies. Where to draw the line between reality and unreality is its greatest problem, which the most recent advocates have done little to solve or even in some cases to recognize.

Malcolm Little, who assumed the names of Malcolm X and El-Hajj Malik El-Shabazz, was perhaps the most remarkable figure as yet produced by the resurgence of black nationalism. His autobiography belongs with the great human documents of our time.[1] His father was a Baptist minister in Omaha, Nebraska, who spent most of his time organizing for Marcus Garvey's UNIA. Malcolm's mother told him that threats from the Ku Klux Klan forced the family to move from Omaha—in which case the local Klansmen did not know that Garvey was the top Klansmen's favorite Negro. Malcolm was one of the "Negroes in the mud" saved by Elijah Muhammad. At the age of twenty-three, serving a ten-year prison sentence for stealing, he received a letter from an older brother "who was forever joining something," saying that he had discovered the "natural religion for the black man." It was the Nation of Islam. His brothers and sisters were converted first. They persuaded Malcolm, still in prison, to believe in Allah and His Messenger. The story of how Malcolm educated himself in prison in an effort to find out how much truth there was in Elijah Muhammad's teachings is infinitely moving; it resembles the once common experience of young workers whose school was the Socialist movement, in which it was often necessary to learn how to read in order to read Marx, Engels, Bebel, or Jaurès.

Once in prison, Malcolm prayed all night to Allah and was rewarded with the fleeting vision of a man with a light-brown skin, an Asiatic countenance, and oily black hair sitting beside his prison bed. Later he came to believe that his phantom visitor had been none other than Master W. D. Fard, the original Messiah. After several years of imprisonment Malcolm was released, joined the Muslim Temple in Detroit, and from there went on to become the Muslim Minister of the New York Temple in 1954. He changed his last name from "Little" to "X," in Muslim fashion, to stand for the African family name which he could never know. By the end of the decade Malcolm rivaled Muhammad in influence and fame, outside if not inside the movement. He was far more quick-witted and sharp-tongued than his teacher and attracted to himself far more publicity, especially from white publications and television programs. Jealousy in Muhammad's entourage and, to some extent, Malcolm's increasing freedom of expression began to estrange them. In March 1964 Malcolm broke with Muhammad and set up a rival group, Muslim Mosque, Inc. After a personal pilgrimage to Mecca and Africa,* he also formed the Organization of Afro-American Unity on a political, nonsectarian basis. While on this pilgrimage he adopted the name of his third incarnation, El-Hajj Malik El-Shabazz, though he continued to be better known as Malcolm X. He was murdered by gunmen as he was addressing a meeting of the OAAU in February 1965, three months before his fortieth birthday.**

---

* In Mecca, the capital of Hejaz in Saudi Arabia, Malcolm was impressed by "the overwhelming spirit of true brotherhood" and the absence of "superiority" and "inferiority" complexes. Wherever he went he was asked questions about America's racial discrimination (*Autobiography*, pp. 339, 344-45). Curiously, he seemed to be oblivious to or at least said nothing about the widespread practice of slavery in Saudi Arabia, which did not *legally* abolish the institution until 1962, when there were an estimated 250,000 black slaves in a population of about eight million.

To make up for his strange silence, one of Malcolm's admirers, the Reverend Albert Cleage, has protested: "He would not have been taken in by what happened in Mecca. Brother Malcolm knew that the Arab Muslims had been the backbone of the slave trade. Those of you who have a sentimental attachment to the 'Black Muslims' in America, or the Muslims that happen to be black, might not like to remember the slave trade with black Africans in Africa was fostered, encouraged, and carried on by the Arab Muslims in Africa. Brother Malcolm knew this. . . . He knew that in Saudi Arabia they are still selling black Africans into slavery, they still make forays into black Africa and bring back black slaves for sale in Arab Muslim countries." (John Henrik Clarke, ed., *Malcolm X: The Man and His Times* [New York: Macmillan, 1969], pp. 15-16.) If Malcolm knew all this, he was, as far as I can make out, careful never to broach it publicly.

** Who killed Malcolm X? Whatever one wants to believe can be found in *Malcolm X: The Man and His Times*. One alleged killer was later identified as Talmadge Hayer, a Black Muslim (pp. 95, 100). Malcolm X himself believed that the Black Muslims were out "to get" him (p. 121). Malcolm X's wife relates that, as early as 1961, Malcolm was told that the Black Muslims "were trying to get rid of him" (p. 139). John Henrik Clarke maintains that Malcolm X was killed by "that invisible, international cartel of power and finance" that also killed Lumumba and Dag Hammarskjöld (p. xxiv). One contributor, James Boggs, asserts that "among black revolutionaries today there is no doubt whatsoever that the CIA engineered his murder because they recognized the grave threat to American Masternationship which this linkup involved" (p. 51). Malcolm X's own followers were so sure that he had been shot by Black Muslims that they had to be restrained from going out and "shooting every Black Muslim that could be found" (p. 97).

One difficulty in assessing what Malcolm X stood for is that, ideologically, there were at least two Malcolm X's—one the orthodox, faithful Muslim follower of Elijah Muhammad, the other an independent leader of his own movement after his break with Muhammad. Malcolm was a follower for twelve years, a leader in his own right for only one. His autobiography was largely written—or told to his collaborator, Alex Haley—in his first phase. It is just as well that this is so or we would never have obtained such a full and vivid self-portrait of Malcolm as a Muslim. In the first two-thirds of the book, then, Malcolm had few if any original ideas to contribute. Whites were still the natural enemies of blacks, and blacks could liberate themselves only by separating themselves totally from whites. In one of his last speeches as a Black Muslim, on November 10, 1963, he told a virtually all-black audience: "We have a common enemy." This common enemy made possible black unity. "And what we have foremost in common is that enemy—the white man. He's an enemy of all of us." [2] But this was almost the last time he spoke this way.

Malcolm first began to re-examine the black-white relationship, according to his own account, in Jedda in the spring of 1964 en route to the holy city of Mecca.[3] "I've had enough of someone else's propaganda," he wrote to a friend. "I'm for the truth, no matter who tells it. I'm for justice, no matter who it is for or against. I'm a human being first and foremost, and as such I'm for whoever and whatever benefits humanity *as a whole*." [4] In effect, he came to distinguish between whites and white racists. In December 1964 he was saying: "They've always said that I'm anti-white. I'm for anybody who's for freedom. I'm for anybody who's for justice. I'm for anybody who's for equality." [5] Later that same month he told a visiting delegation: "That doesn't mean we're against white people, but we sure are against the Ku Klux Klan and the White Citizens Councils; and anything that looks like it's against us, we're against it." [6] In speech after speech, he tried to clarify his new position: "I don't speak against the sincere, well-meaning, good white people. I have learned that not all white people are racists. I am speaking against and my fight is against the white *racists*. I firmly believe that Negroes have the right to fight against these racists, by any means that are necessary." [7]

A somewhat similar development took place in his conception of black nationalism. In his November 10, 1963, speech he defined nationalism in relatively simple and clear terms: "When you want a nation, that's called nationalism." He chose to emphasize two things about every revolution—land and bloodshed. "Look at the American Revolution in 1776," he said. "That revolution was for what? For land. Why did they want land? Independence. How was it carried out? Bloodshed. Number one, it was based on land, the basis of independence. And the only way they could get it was bloodshed." He reduced the French, the Russian, and the Chinese revolutions to the same factors. Of the two, however, he made "land" primary. "Revolution is based on land," he held. "Land is the basis of all independence. Land is the basis of freedom, justice, and equality." [8]

But where was the land of *his* people, and *his* revolution? In his last speech as a Black Muslim on December 1, 1963, he took the position that it would be best for "the twenty-two million ex-slaves [to be sent] *back to our own homeland*" in Africa, but if the white United States government was "afraid" of doing that, then "America must set aside some separate territory here in the Western Hemisphere, where the two races can live apart from each other." [9] He continued to take this line even after his break with the Muslims. In March 1964, in his first press conference on his own, he still swore allegiance to what he thought was Elijah Muhammad's solution—"complete separation, with our people going back home, to our own African homeland." [10] He justified this course by transmuting the twenty-two million African-Americans into "Africans who are in America." He once exclaimed: "You're nothing but Africans. Nothing but Africans." [11] In early 1964, then, the land he had in mind for his nation and his revolution was primarily Africa, and his program amounted to old-fashioned emigrationism.

Another reason he gave for identifying with Africa was numerical. As long as African-Americans, as he called them at this time, were only twenty-two million in a population almost ten times as many, they were a small minority. By internationalizing the American Negro struggle, he saw a way of turning the minority into a majority. He talked himself into the notion that "today, power is international, real power is international; today real power is not local." (What evidently impressed him most was the efflorescence of African votes at international conferences—as if such conferences did much more than vote or had the power to enforce their votes.) This line of reasoning led him to be utterly defeatist about the prospect of American Negroes within the context of the United States alone. "If your power base is only here, you can forget it," he said brusquely. "You can't build a power base here." And he advised: "You can work here, but you'd better put your base somewhere else." [12]

In a matter of months, then, Malcolm moved from American black nationalism to African black internationalism. By ostensibly "internationalizing" the American Negro struggle, he shifted its land base from America to Africa. Even so, he could not hold on very long to blackness as the unifying element. In Africa itself, he was astonished to learn that it was not all black, just as he had previously learned that the real Muslim world was not all black.[13] He liked to tell the story of his talk with the Algerian ambassador in Ghana in May 1964: "When I told him that my political, social and economic philosophy was black nationalism, he asked me very frankly, well, where did that leave him? Because he was white. He was an African, but he was Algerian, and to all appearances he was a white man. And he said if I define my objective as the victory of black nationalism, where does that leave him? Where does that leave revolutionaries in Morocco, Egypt, Iraq, Mauritania?" [14] Forced to choose between Africa and blackness, Malcolm at first chose Africa—all of it, black and white. In fact, he could not hold in harness the three chief factors which he thought went into his revolutionary make-up—that he was a Moslem, a transplanted African, and a black. Black nationalism was not big enough to contain all Moslems and all Africans, and he refused to settle for a black Moslem or a black African revolution only.

Month after month in his last year, he continued to redefine away his original presuppositions. As long as he emphasized the land as the all-important component in any nationalism, he seemed to imply that he was committed to a physical emigrationism. But in one of his letters from Ghana in May 1964, he shifted over to what was clearly a psychological emigrationism. "Just as the American Jew is in harmony (politically, economically and culturally) with world Jewry," he wrote, "it is time for all African-Americans to become an integral part of the world's Pan-Africanists, and even though we might remain in America physically while fighting for the benefits the Constitution guarantees us, we must 'return' to Africa philosophically and culturally and develop a working unity in their framework of Pan-Africanism." By the end of that year he made explicit the distinction between physical and psychological emigrationism: "And I believe this, that if we migrated back to Africa culturally, philosophically and psychologically, while remaining here physically, the spiritual bond that would develop between us and Africa through this cultural, philosophical migration, so-called migration, would enhance our position here, because we would have our contacts with them acting as roots or foundations behind us." He added in his old vein: "You never will have a foundation in America." [15]

This position was also highly vulnerable. If his analogy

with the American Jews meant anything, it could not be reconciled with an indigenous black nationalism in the sense that he had previously given it—"when you want a nation." For American Jews had never thought of themselves as constituting "a nation within a nation." At most the analogy might suggest that American Negroes had to find a way to maintain a viable balance between their "double consciousness" as Americans and as Negroes, just as the Jews had to come to terms with their Americanism and their Jewishness. Moreover, Malcolm seemed to envisage another type of double consciousness in which Negroes would live in America physically and in Africa psychologically. In his enthusiasm for Africa, he forgot—or chose to deny—that a people's culture was ultimately rooted in a native habitation, in their everyday lives, in their work and experiences. His division of the physical and the psychological was unrealistically schematic, designed to get him over a difficult transition period from one type of black nationalism to another—or none.

Malcolm saw that he had cut the ground from under his nationalism of only a year before. As early as his April 3, 1964, speech, just before his first pilgrimage to Mecca, he had defined his black nationalism in a curiously all-embracing way that took in everything from the Student Nonviolent Coordinating Committee (SNCC) to the National Association for the Advancement of Colored People (NAACP). "The political philosophy of black nationalism means that the black man should control the politics and the politicians in his own community; no more." [16] This formula was vague enough to mean anything or nothing; yet "control" of politics and politicians might be achieved without a revolution, especially if such control was exemplified by the NAACP; and "community" was a far more localized and politically neutral term than "nation."

In the final chapter of his autobiography, he still remarked that "a *true* Negro revolt might entail, for instance, fighting for separate black states within this country—which several groups and individuals have advocated, long before Elijah Muhammad." Yet a few pages later he defined the mission of his newly formed Organization of Afro-American Unity in quite different terms. It was, he said, "an all-black organization whose ultimate objective was to help create a society in which there could exist honest white-black brotherhood." [17] The two programmatic statements that he composed for the organization say hardly more than, as in the first, "We will support the aspirations of our people for brotherhood and solidarity in a larger unity transcending all organizational differences," or, as in the second, "We are not opposed to multi-ethnic associations in any walk of life," but Afro-American unity is a necessary precondition for beneficial "ethnic intermingling." [18]

In the end, Malcolm went all the way. On January 19, 1965, a month before his death, he was asked on television: "But you no longer believe in a black state?" Malcolm replied decisively: "No." He was asked again: "In North America?" He replied: "No, I believe in a society in which people can live like human beings on the basis of equality." In an interview which appeared after his death, he called the attention of the interviewer to the fact that he had not been using the expression "black nationalism" for several months. Then he added: "But I still would be hard pressed to give a specific definition of the over-all philosophy which I think is necessary for the liberation of the black people in this country." [19]

Thus, in his last phase, Malcolm was far less interested in a separate African-American nation than in some type of revolutionary internationalism, the exact nature of which was still hazy to him at the time of his death. He was drawn to the Trotskyists without sharing all their presuppositions. Of the two basic elements with which he had started out—land and bloodshed—he held on to the second far more tenaciously and consistently than to the first. Yet even here he left himself open to misunderstanding and misuse by those who wished to exploit him for their own ends. In his April 3, 1964, speech, he specifically advocated using ballots as well as bullets, whichever might be necessary. "Don't be throwing out any ballots," he counseled. "A ballot is like a bullet. You don't throw your ballots until you see a target, and if that target is not within your reach, keep your ballot in your pocket." On January 7, 1965, he stated publicly: "I believe in political action, yes. Whatever kind of action is necessary. When you hear me say 'by any means necessary,' I mean exactly that. I believe in anything that is necessary to correct unjust conditions—political, economic, social, physical, anything that's necessary. I believe in it—as long as it's intelligently directed and designed to get results." [20] Those who take the phrase "by any means necessary" to mean that only violent means are necessary—just as those who twist it in favor of only non-violent means—are not doing justice to Malcolm X's more mature political subtlety, complexity—and perplexity.

In effect, the nationalist legacy of Malcolm X is extremely problematic and ambiguous. A Trotskyist writer, George Breitman, who has made a careful and useful study of Malcolm's last year, contends that "he was becoming black nationalist plus revolutionary." [21] But by black nationalist in the final stage, Breitman can mean little more than that Malcolm wanted to solve black problems first, not that he had anything more to do with black American nationhood or Back-to-Africa-ism. His intense emphasis on ties with black Africa as the "motherland" was, however, culturally and politically related to the old Back-to-Africa emigrationism. Indeed, to the extent that he related Afro-American liberation in particular to African liberation in general, he might be said to be an exponent of a kind of international black revolutionary emigrationism. He was primarily an inspired agitator, not an original ideologist, and he picked up bits and pieces of what he considered to be useful ideological baggage as he went along. Those who take his name in vain to advance their own favorite revolutionary recipes do his memory no service. He left his own best epitaph: "My whole life had been a chronology of—*changes*." [22]

The Black Panthers

7

The Black Panthers, perhaps the most interesting and influential of the present-day purely political nationalist movements, have also had trouble with the concepts of a black "colony" and "nation" in the United States. They have tried to cope with the difficulties in still another way.

The Black Panther Party was formed in Oakland, California, in October 1966 by two young black nationalists, Huey P. Newton, then twenty-five, and Bobby Seale, five years older. The guiding spirit and dominant personality was—and is—Newton. His family, which he once described as "lower class, working class," moved from Louisiana, where he was born, the youngest of seven children, to California. He was graduated from two-year Merritt College, in Oakland, where he met Seale. At the school they took their first step toward nationalist political activity by joining a local Afro-American Association, which soon proved insufficiently militant for them. Newton wanted to become a lawyer, Seale an actor. About a year at San Francisco Law School convinced Newton that he was not cut out to be a lawyer. Seale spent almost four years in the Army, the last six months in the stockade because, he later claimed, "I opposed racism in the top brass, [in] a lieutenant-colonel," and he was given a "bad conduct discharge" one month before the end of his four-year term. He then drifted from odd job to odd job without getting very far in his chosen career.

One evening, during an argument at a party, Newton slashed a black auto worker with a steak knife and spent eight months in jail for the assault. After his release he and Seale got together again, and, according to one version, Seale stimulated his renewed political activity by giving him *The Wretched of the Earth* by Frantz Fanon to read.* When some of their younger friends at Merritt formed a Soul Students Advisory Council to demand a "black curriculum," they took an interest in it.

An incident in Berkeley apparently led them to go much further. It seems that a white policeman tried to arrest Seale

* Fanon is another author who might be read more carefully by some black nationalists in America. Of the first congress of the African Cultural Society held in Paris in 1956, he wrote: "But little by little the American Negroes realized that the essential problems confronting them were not the same as those that confronted the African Negroes. The Negroes of Chicago only resemble the Nigerians or the Tanganyikans in so far as they were all defined in relation to the whites. But once the first comparisons had been made and subjective feelings were assuaged, the American Negroes realized that the objective problems were fundamentally heterogeneous. . . . Negritude therefore finds its first limitation in the phenomena which take account of the formation of the historical character of men. Negro and African–Negro culture broke up into different entities because the men who wished to incarnate these cultures realized that every culture is first and foremost national, and that the problems which kept Richard Wright or Langston Hughes on the alert were fundamentally different from those which might confront Leopold Senghor or Jomo Kenyatta" (*The Wretched of the Earth* [New York: Grove Press, 1965], p. 216).

for reciting poems from a chair at an outdoor café, thereby blocking the sidewalk. A fight ensued; no one was arrested. But Newton and Seale thereupon decided to give up the Soul Students Advisory Council and to form a broader organization called the Black Panther Party for Self-Defense. (The panther reference came from the symbol of the Lowndes County Freedom Organization that had been launched in Alabama six months earlier.) The name was later shortened to Black Panther Party to emphasize a larger goal than "self-defense." While working in the Poverty Office in Oakland in October 1966, they wrote a 10-Point Platform and Program for the new party.[1]

The Panthers seemed at first little more than another self-appointed local band of black nationalists in an urban ghetto. Their chief claims to publicity were their armed patrols, which drove through the streets of Oakland, and their mannerism of saying "right on" as often as possible.* Their first important convert early in 1967 was Eldridge Cleaver, author of *Soul on Ice,* who, like Malcolm X, had been converted to Elijah Muhammad's Black Muslims in prison and had sided with Malcolm X after the latter's break with them. Newton impressed Cleaver, who was then working for *Ramparts,* by leading a group of armed Panthers into the office of the magazine and daring a policeman to shoot him. The police flinched that time, but in a shoot-out in Oakland in October 1967, Newton was wounded, one policeman was killed, another was wounded, and Newton was given a two-to-fifteen-year sentence for manslaughter.

From this unlikely beginning, the Black Panthers have

---

* "Well, its time for us right now to decide what we're gonna do, where we gone do it, how we gone do it, and when we gone do it. If you ain't decided whether if you gone do it, then go on home, right on. Because when we say free Huey, that's only the first step to freeing all people. . . . Huey's gonna be set free or nobody gone be free, right. Right on. If Huey can't be free what goddamn bit of difference does it make if you're free, right on. FREE HUEY NOW." (Kathleen Cleaver at the May Day, 1969, rally in San Francisco, *The Black Panther,* May 11, 1969, p. 11.)

become a formidable national movement. In three years they claimed to have set up about thirty chapters, the largest in the Oakland–San Francisco area and Chicago, which may have had a membership of about five thousand at its peak, but this was probably cut to about half or less by the end of 1969 as a result of police persecution.[2] Besides Cleaver, it was able to win over, though only for a short time, such well-known figures as H. Rap Brown and Stokely Carmichael of SNCC. It entered into a coalition with the white-based Peace and Freedom Party, which ran Cleaver for President in the 1968 election. Its program of black nationalism was endorsed by the Students for a Democratic Society in March 1969, and it precipitated the SDS split in June that same year. It is allied with a new League of Revolutionary Black Workers, which has sprung up in the automobile industry and particularly threatens the United Auto Workers Union. It initially provided much of the inspiration, leadership, and program of the black student unions in universities, colleges, and high schools.

The Black Panther ideology, which is all that concerns us here, is only partially revealed by the official platform and rules. Point 1 of the 10-Point Platform and Program adopted in October 1966 reads: "We want freedom. We want power to determine the destiny of our Black Community." Other points call for full employment, decent housing, education, and the liberation of all black prisoners from all prisons and jails. Point 10, the most nationalistic, states: "We want land, bread, housing, education, clothing, justice, and peace. And as our major political objective, a United Nations-supervised plebiscite to be held throughout the black colony in which only black colonial subjects will be allowed to participate, for the purpose of determining the will of the black people as to their national destiny." The rest of the document hints at the meaning of this demand by quoting the justification for secession in the Declaration of Independence of 1776.

But this was hardly a fully thought-out program of black nationhood. It left the decision to a vaguely formulated plebiscite, and, even if the "black colony" decided to "dissolve the political bands" connecting it to the existing United States, it did not suggest what the next step might be.[3]

The full Black Panther ideology emerges only in the pages of its official organ, *The Black Panther,* published weekly in Berkeley, California, and especially in the articles, speeches, and interviews of its main leaders. Some early columns by Newton in 1967, before he was imprisoned, have been collected in a little pamphlet. These essays show that Newton's basic ideas were formed before his shoot-out with the Oakland police and derived mainly from Fanon, Malcolm X, Mao Tse-tung, and Fidel Castro.

For Newton, the "Black colony of Afro-America" has a unique and universal mission. "The Black people in America are the only people who can free the world, loosen the yoke of colonialism, and destroy the war machine." No other country can defeat this "monster" as long as it continues to function. "But Black people can make a malfunction of this machine from within." In order to do so, however, "They must have the basic tool of liberation: the gun"—a lesson attributed to Mao Tse-tung and Malcolm X. Guerrilla warfare is the tactical method that goes with the basic tool. As a self-styled "Vanguard Party," the Black Panthers do not think they have to do the whole job by themselves. They need only set an example and the masses will follow. Newton's own example leaves little to the imagination: "When the masses hear that a gestapo policeman has been executed while sipping coffee at a counter, and the revolutionary executioners fled without being traced, the masses will see the validity of this type of approach to resistance." The pamphlet, however, tells little about the ultimate objective beyond proposing that "Black people must now move, from the grassroots up through the perfumed circles of the Black bourgeoisie, to seize by any means necessary a proportionate share of the power vested and collected in the structure of America." [4]

Since 1967 Black Panther ideology has become a more fully developed, if not essentially different, system. In essence, it is a hybrid made up of revolutionary black nationalism and what is by now an old friend, "Marxism-Leninism." As a result, it is not quite like any other black nationalism or any other Marxism-Leninism. For example, no other "Marxist-Leninists" have ever identified themselves with the *Lumpenproletariat,* the most rootless and degraded elements in capitalist society, whom Marx and Engels regarded as a "dangerous class" whose conditions of life destined it to play a reactionary role.* The peculiar "amalgam," as Trotsky would have called it, of bits and pieces from Frantz Fanon, Malcolm X, Mao Tse-tung, Ernesto Che Guevara, Régis Debray, and others, is typical of the kind of do-it-yourself Marxism-Leninism that has come into vogue.** It is

* A statement by Chief of Staff David Hilliard was headed, "Lumpen-Proletarian Discipline Versus Bourgeois Reactionism," the former representing the Panther ideal (*The Black Panther,* August 9, 1969, p. 11). Later Hilliard wrote of "our duty as revolutionaries, as members of the lumpen proletariat (field niggers)" (*ibid.,* September 6, 1969, p. 2).

Huey Newton's brother Melvin has recalled that Huey from the outset "saw the Panthers even then as a potential mass movement, something that the *Lumpenproletariat* could relate to. Huey had a lot of confidence in the *Lumpenproletariat;* he believed it could be rallied to its own cause." (Gene Marine, *The Black Panthers* [New York: New American Library, 1969], p. 37.)

In *The Communist Manifesto* of 1848, Marx and Engels referred to the *Lumpenproletariat* as follows: "The 'dangerous class,' the social scum, that passively rotting mass thrown off by the lowest layers of old society, may, here and there, be swept into the movement by a proletarian revolution; its conditions of life, however, prepare it far more for the part of a bribed tool of reactionary intrigue" (Section I: "Bourgeois and Proletarians"). I know of no other self-styled Marxist or Marxist-Leninist group which has ever before tried to glorify the *Lumpenproletariat.*

** The Panthers are nothing if not catholic in their revolutionary taste. To the list above should be added Lumumba, Garvey, Ho Chi Minh, as well as Marx, Lenin, Stalin, and Trotsky, judging from the following testimonials:

especially characteristic of movements which have invited themselves into the Marxist-Leninist tradition from the outside, bringing with them their own national or particularist folkways, and shopping among all the current versions of the doctrine for those features or formulas which happen to suit or please them the most. In this respect Black Pantherism resembles Castroism but has gone much further in asserting its individuality.

Organizationally the party also shows its hybrid make-up. It is headed by a Central Committee, a term traditionally used in the Communist movement. But unlike such parties, which are headed by Secretaries or General Secretaries, the Panthers' No. 1 leader is the Minister of Defense—Huey P.

George Murray: "Our thinking is inspired by Che Guevara, Malcolm X, Lumumba, Ho Chi Minh and Mao Tse-tung" (*The Black Panther*, October 12, 1968, p. 14).

Huey P. Newton: "Brother Mao put that quite well, and we will follow the thoughts of Chairman Mao" (*ibid.*, March 3, 1969, p. 2).

Field Marshal D. C. [Don Cox]: "And we dig on all the people that held up the light before: Marx, Lenin, Stalin, Mao, Fidel, Che, Lumumba and Malcolm. And we dig on all the people who are holding up the light now, Ho Chi Minh, those brothers and sisters in Al Fatah, those bad Palestinian Guerrillas, those comrades in arms in Asia and Latin America" (*ibid.*, April 20, 1969, p. 16).

Bobby Seale: "You got your Red Books, hold your Red Books up and tell the brothers where we getting some new ideology from. We're saying like Huey P. Newton said, 'that we're going to follow the thoughts of Chairman Mao'" (*ibid.*, May 11, 1969, p. 11).

Ray "Masai" Hewitt: "We dig Chairman Mao, Ho Chi Minh, we have a profound love for Fidel Castro" (*ibid.*, May 31, 1969, p. 16).

For Trotsky, see below, pp. 112–13n.

As for supporting Al Fatah, the Panthers are so anti-Israel that their organ attempted to justify the assassination of Senator Robert Kennedy rather than President Richard Nixon or California's Governor Ronald Reagan on the ground that "Kennedy was a fence-sitter on the Middle East situation" whereas "the Nixons and Reagans are consistent, open fascists." *The Black Panther* explained: "But when a liberal asks for respect from third world people by 'helping' and then deceives them by representing enemy interests, the liberal can expect a retaliation" ("Sirhan—A Revolutionary," *ibid.*, March 23, 1969, p. 14).

Toward the end of 1969, *The Black Panther*'s favorite foreign Communist seemed to be Kim Il Sung, President of North Korea, judging from the space allotted to his statements and speeches.

Newton. The idea that the top leadership should reside in the military commander, who simultaneously fulfills the chief political role, derives directly from Régis Debray. After Newton comes Bobby Seale, the Chairman, reminiscent of Mao Tse-tung's favorite title. The next in line is the Minister of Information, Eldridge Cleaver (in absentia). No. 4 is the Chief of Staff, David Hilliard, an ex-longshoreman. The Central Committee also contains a Field Marshal, Don Cox; a Minister of Education, Ray "Masai" Hewitt; a Minister of Foreign Affairs (unnamed); a Minister of Justice (unnamed); a Prime Minister (unnamed); a Communications Secretary, Kathleen Cleaver, wife of Eldridge Cleaver; and a Minister of Culture, Emory Douglas, who is also the party's Revolutionary Artist.* With Newton in prison and Cleaver in exile, the two main leaders have been Seale and Hilliard. Local Panther groups duplicate the national set-up with a Deputy Chief of Staff and Deputy Ministers.

What is most individual about the Black Panthers is, of course, what concerns them most—the "national liberation" of the "black colony" in the "white mother country." The last term was apparently originated by Eldridge Cleaver— probably out of Frantz Fanon, who also used the term "mother country" for the French colonial regime.[5] It indicates the difference between the Panthers and the Back-to-Africa nationalists. The mother country of the Panthers' black colony is white America, not Africa. Since the mother country is not Africa, there is no reason to go back to it. Without denying the existence of vestigial ties with Africa,

* On February 11, 1968, Eldridge Cleaver announced publicly that the Black Panthers and SNCC had "worked out a merger." SNCC sources claimed that he went too far and that the two groups had merely formed an "alliance." In any case, three SNCC leaders were appointed to leading posts in the Panthers' Central Committee—Stokely Carmichael as Prime Minister, H. Rap Brown as Minister of Justice, and James Forman as Minister of Foreign Affairs. Brown and Forman resigned from their posts in August 1968, Carmichael in July 1969. For a version of the Panthers-SNCC tie-up and possible misunderstanding, see Julius Lester, *Revolutionary Notes* (New York: Richard W. Baron, 1969), pp. 144–49.

the Panthers strongly reject and oppose the Back-to-Africa line even in an attenuated form, which they contemptuously call "cultural nationalism."

Newton has sternly disapproved of the return to African culture:

> Cultural nationalism deals with a return to the old culture of Africa and that we are somehow freed by identifying and returning to this culture, to the African cultural stage of the 1100's or before then. Somehow they [cultural nationalists] believe that they will be free through identifying in this manner. As far as we are concerned, we believe that it's important for us to recognize our origins and to identify with the revolutionary Black people of Africa and people of color throughout the world. But as far as returning per se to the ancient customs, we don't see any necessity in this.[6]

Other Panther leaders have been less polite. Former Minister of Education George Mason Murray has called this kind of pro-African cultural nationalism "a fixation in a people's development like a half-formed baby," "reactionary and insane and counterrevolutionary," "a bourgeois-capitalist scheme, to confuse the masses of people, so that they will not assault the city halls, the bank tellers, and managers, or seize control of community schools." [7] A programmatic article in *The Black Panther* ridiculed the "fools running around who declare that they are 'just trying to be black' by wearing dashikis and bubas and who tell black people that they should relate to African customs and African heritage that we left three hundred years ago, that this will make them free, that reading black history will make them better." [8]

Ironically, therefore, the Panthers have decided that the emphasis on Black Studies programs has gone too far. In May 1969 Minister of Education Ray "Masai" Hewitt denounced Black Studies as a "new trick bag." He told of having talked with "many brothers from Africa" who "are not hung up on Swahili or Arabic." Of the new vogue for the "natural head," he reported: "Very few of the African brothers that we met had what could be called a 'Natural Head.' They just had hair. You couldn't call it one of those custom-tailored natural heads. They never spoke Swahili and every time we told them that there were brothers here studying Swahili for the revolution, they burst out laughing." He added: "The movement toward Black Studies in colleges and other Black cultural programs have become a fixation. At one point in the revolutionary development of our people it was a revolutionary step. Instead of taking it as a beginning step many cultural nationalist opportunist bootlicking cowards and freaks have latched onto it." [9]

The nationalist side of the Panthers' ideology makes them emphasize black unity; the "Marxist-Leninist" side makes them emphasize a social revolution by both blacks and whites. Unlike other nationalist groups, the Panthers do not believe that the "black colony" can liberate itself alone. "We have two evils to fight, capitalism and racism," Newton says. "We must destroy both racism and capitalism." [10] The Panthers realize that they cannot destroy capitalism and install socialism in the black community without destroying capitalism and installing socialism in the white community. As a programmatic statement put it: "There must be a revolution in the white mother country, led by white radicals and poor whites, and national liberation in the black and third world colony here in America. We can't triumph in the colony alone because that is just like cutting one finger off a hand. It still functions, you dig it. No, when we deal with this monster we must deal with it totally." [11]

This suggests that the Panthers expect the black nationalist revolution to be part of, or accompanied by, a larger white social revolution. In this respect, therefore, they do not belong in the line of pure black nationalist movements, such as Garvey's. In fact, by the summer of 1969, Newton seemed to be appealing to all "people," not merely to black people. In a significant restatement of his party's position in a Negro magazine of mass circulation, he immediately struck a populist, rather than a nationalist, note: "The Black Panther Party is the people's party. We are fundamentally interested in one thing, that is, freeing all people from all forms of slavery in order that every man will be his own master." He blamed capitalism for all that was wrong, and made socialism the precondition for freedom of any kind, including self-determination. "All members of the working class must seize the means of production," he wrote. "This, naturally, includes black people." He might have added that this, naturally, includes even more white people.[12]

Though the Black Panthers have remained a purely black organization, its leaders have found a way around that restriction too. In July 1969 they sponsored a National Conference for a United Front Against Fascism in Oakland, California, out of which came local National Committees to Combat Fascism. One black nationalist organ noted caustically that over 90 per cent of those attending the Oakland conference were white.[13] These National Committees were designed to take in whites, especially those who, as Chairman Seale put it, had been asking why they could not join the Panther Party. "We see the National Committees as the political organizing bureaus of the Black Panther Party," Seale declared.[14] In another period these committees might have been called front organizations, but something was different—this was a black movement with a white front instead of a white movement with a black front. At the conference itself, Seale also disclosed that the Panthers favored creating a "new party, the new workers' party, or what have you," on the model of the "liberation fronts" in Africa and Latin America, "an American Liberation Front composed of all the people of this nation." [15] The National Committees were presumably conceived as "organizing bureaus" of the new party as well as of the Black Panther Party.

Thus the Panthers had changed in three short years from a largely black nationalist organization to a black revolu-

tionary organization, and the latter in turn had led it to become a black organization with white appendages. At the Oakland conference and elsewhere, Panther leaders have made it clear that they consider themselves to be the vanguard of the social as well as of the nationalist revolution. Those white organizations which recognize their leadership must expect the treatment meted out to the Students for a Democratic Society at the Oakland conference. When the SDS delegates objected to the Panther proposal for "community control of the police," they were given a dose of the special brand of Pantherite polemics. Seale called them "those little bourgeois, snooty nose motherfucking SDS's." *
Only that faction in the SDS which was willing to accept this type of "criticism" and come back for more was permitted to remain in the Panthers' good graces.

The Panthers' relations with various white organizations and groups have varied from time to time. At the Oakland conference the Panthers found the official American Communist Party most useful, and a well-known party intellectual, Dr. Herbert Aptheker, who has specialized in Ameri-

---

* Panther political style is *sui generis*. In his rebuke of the SDS, Seale continued: "And that we're gonna kick their motherfucking ass, if they don't freeze on their shit, and we want to make that clear to them. . . . And we'll beat those little sissies, those little school boy's ass if they don't try to straighten up their politics. So we want to make that known to SDS and the first motherfucker that gets out of order had better stand in line for some kind of disciplinary actions from the Black Panther Party" (*The Black Panther*, August 9, 1969, p. 12).

Another Panther leader, Virgil Morell, once defined the revolution as follows: "The only way we can do this is to pick up the gun. We are gonna walk all across this motherfucking government and say Stick 'em up, motherfuckers—this is a hold up: we come to get everything that belongs to us" (*ibid.*, October 12, 1968, p. 5).

And in an order purging nineteen members from the Jersey City branch: "The Party will no longer tolerate these counterrevolutionary m—f—s, who by their deeds are harming the interest of the Party and the People. These degenerates have aroused the anger of the people, 'the people will kill them, and we gonna kill every m—f— who went along with their s—t" (*ibid.*, May 4, 1969, p. 7). The language of "Marxism-Leninism" was never like this.

can Negro history, was permitted to make an interminable theoretical address to the meeting. Seale later explained that the American Communists had taken the Panthers' criticism to heart and had done more work for the conference than any other white organization.* Despite these good marks for the American Communists, the Panthers' favorite white revolutionary group has continued to be the Young Patriots, a band of transplanted young Southerners located in Chicago. Another Chicago-based group, the Young Lords Organization, originally a street gang in a Puerto Rican community, has also been recognized by the Panthers as authentically revolutionary. A Chinese-American "Red Guard" in San Francisco has copied the Panthers' style and program, and there is an American Indian satellite group known as NARP.

This Pantherite shift in line—or, at least, in emphasis—was primarily behind the resignation of Stokely Carmichael. In June 1967, Carmichael had been the beneficiary of Executive Mandate (as Minister of Defense Newton's early pronunciamentos were called) No. 2. In recognition of his distinguished services "in the struggle for the total liberation of Black people from oppression in racist white America," it had invested him with the rank of Field Marshal.[16] In February 1968 Carmichael was elevated to the largely ornamental post of Prime Minister. But Carmichael had come into the Panthers from SNCC, which he had purged of all whites during his chairmanship. He never seems to have been reconciled to the Panthers' idea of coalition with white organizations, let alone a black-white social revolution, and the break on this issue came in July 1969. From his self-

* Seale's exact words were: "And that's just a fascist pig tactic to try to say that the Black Panther Party is led by the Communist Party, and we're not against Communism—we dig Communism. And we have criticisms of the American Communist Party, and lately they're relating to the criticism because we told them they had to put more things into practice, and it seems that they did better than some of the other organizations, because they actually came out and did some degree of work to put the conference over, when we sat down and talked to them" (*The Black Panther,* August 9, 1969, p. 13).

imposed "exile" in Guinea, Carmichael charged that the Panthers were "dogmatic, dishonest, vicious and in collusion with whites"—of which derelictions the latter was probably the least forgivable. Carmichael charged: "The alliances formed by the party are alliances which I cannot politically agree with, because the history of Africans living in the U.S. has shown that any premature alliance with white radicals has led to complete subversion of blacks by the whites through their direct or indirect control of the black organization." [17] Cleaver answered for the Panthers that "you cats in SNCC" suffered from a "paranoid fear" of whites because they had had to wrest control of their organization from whites, unlike the Panthers who had never been in that situation.[18] In fact, the difference between them was not so much that of white control of black organizations as of a black-against-white nationalist revolution *versus* a black-and-white social-plus-nationalist revolution. The Panthers' "coalitions" with whites have thus far been arranged on the Panthers' terms, though Carmichael obviously doubted that they could continue to have their way in a white-black mass movement "of all the people of this nation." Once Carmichael broke away from the Panthers, he was denounced as nothing more than "a running dog and a lackey." [19]

The loss of Carmichael to the Panthers was less important for the man than for the policy he represented. The Carmichael-Cleaver dispute reminded one black nationalist editor of the Garvey–Du Bois feud almost fifty years earlier.[20] In both cases, pure-and-simple black nationalism that totally rejected whites was opposed by a more complex and social-minded black nationalism that linked the fates of black and white. In this sense, a historic rift in black nationalism was taking a new but no less irreconcilable form.

Nevertheless, the membership of the Panthers is wholly black, and for that reason they may stand or fall on the persuasiveness of their black nationalist program. Yet it is precisely in this area that they are ideologically most vague and uncertain.

The original proposal in the Platform and Program of October 1966—to hold a United Nations-supervised plebiscite —was clearly an evasion of the issue. It is, of course, highly improbable that the UN would or could hold such a plebiscite; at best the proposal passed the problem on to the black voters; and it did not tell them how the Panthers wanted them to vote. There is reason to believe that this evasiveness was deliberate and that the Panther strategists considered any more concrete position premature. At a Peace and Freedom Party forum on February 11, 1968, Cleaver remarked: "It's very important to realize that in moving to gain power, you do not conceal or repudiate the land question, you hold it in abeyance. What you're saying is that we must first get ourselves organized, and then we can get some of this land." [21] Since then, the Panther leaders seem to have had a hard time making up their minds. In an early phase Newton would go no further than: "Our problem is unity at this point. We have to unify ourselves. We can handle the colony better than anyone else. We are a colonized people. Many Black communities are like decentralized colonies throughout this country." [22] But what this implied for black American nationhood he did not say.

A later effort by Chairman Seale at the Anti-Fascist Conference in Oakland in July 1969 was also somewhat tantalizing if seemingly more definite:

> We are not saying that self-determination of the black people in the black communities is not correct. It is necessary. But we are not saying that black people are a nation just because they are black. We are saying that black people are a nation because they have the same economic oppression that they are subjected to; because they have, number two, a basic psychological make-up in how they react to that environment they exist in; third, because they describe

what's happening; because black people in the black community, understanding genocide (with number 4 coming up) that the language, psychological make-up, economic conditions and the (4) geographical location that black people exist in, generally defined as ghettos. The geographical location defines, with all four of those points, black people as a nation, defines Mexican American people as a nation where they are. Whether they're split or divided because we are colonialized, because the Third World people are colonialized. That's what defines a nation. We are not basing it on racism. We understand nationalism in terms of what a nation is, and we understand internationalism.[23] *

Whatever may be thought of Seale's reasons, this statement seemed to commit him to the proposition that there was a black nation in the United States, as well as a Mexican American nation, even if they were made up of congeries of far-flung ghettos. Soon afterward, Chief of Staff Hilliard added a new note for which he may go down in history as the originator of a genuinely novel concept in the annals of international socialism. He was talking about the SDS opposition to the Pantherite demand for community control or decentralization of the police when it occurred to him to say: "To decentralize the community imperialists, and implement probably on just the community level—Socialism. And that's probably too Marxist-Leninist for those motherfuckers to understand, but we think that Stalin was very clear in this concept—that socialism could be implemented in one country, we say that it can be implemented in one community." [24]

And so, if Stalin could have "socialism in one country," the Panthers, if their Chief of Staff can be trusted, see no reason why they cannot have "socialism in one community." **

* I have thought it best to give Seale's statement in his own words. *The Black Panther*'s practice of publishing verbatim texts of verbal statements makes for colorful if sometimes confusing reading.

** This is not the first time that Hilliard invoked the name of Stalin. He

After all this, however, the Panthers' maximum leader, Huey P. Newton, in August 1969, explicitly referred to the blacks in America as a "national minority" and, inferentially, as an "ethnic minority," not a nation. He demanded the freedom "to structure our own communities so that we can determine the institutions of the community that will perpetuate our culture." [25] But it would clearly make a difference to that structure if it were based on the concept of a nation or merely of a national minority.

A month later Newton also decided to change his mind—or at least his "rhetoric"—on what being "colonized" meant. "At one time I thought that only Blacks were colonized," he announced. "But I think we have to change our rhetoric to an extent because the whole American people have been colonized, if you view exploitation as a colonized effect, now they're exploited." [26] In effect, Newton had decided to equate "colonization" with "exploitation." Inasmuch as the whole American people were to his mind "exploited," they were at the same time "colonized," and his change in "rhetoric" enlarged the formerly "black colony" to take in the entire American population. But this virtually emptied the concept of an internal American "colony" of all specific content. If "colonization" means nothing more than "exploitation," there is really no need of the former term. Far from making the concept of "colony" more inclusive, the concept of "exploitation" swallows it up altogether.

At about the same time, Newton argued that even a separate black America of five or six states could not survive if the rest of the United States remained capitalistic. "We also

---

had previously "discovered" Stalin, Lenin, and Trotsky in the following way: "Our whole thing about discovering the triumvirate consisting of Lenin, Trotsky, and Stalin. It is just a matter of trying to give a very complete picture of history. . . . The reason that they fear Joseph Stalin is because of the distorted facts that they have gained through the Western press. The one thing that we respect about Stalin, is that Stalin was able to capture the will of the people" (*The Black Panther,* April 20, 1969, p. 18). One wonders whether Stalin or Trotsky would be the more displeased by the company he was made to keep.

take into consideration the fact that if Blacks at this very minute were able to secede the union, and say have five states, or six states [*sic*]. It would be impossible to function in freedom side by side with a capitalistic imperialistic country." He implied that enclaves and ghettos made for good "strategy" but might not make for good nationhood: "In other words we're not really handling this question at this time because we feel that for us that it is somewhat premature, that I realize the physiological value of fighting for a territory. But at this time the Black Panther Party feels that we don't want to be in an enclave type situation where we would be more isolated than we already are now. We're isolated in the ghetto areas, and we think this is a very good location as far as strategy is concerned, as far as waging a strong battle against the established order." [27]

The Panther ideologists, if they can be called that, have thus struggled not too successfully with the "nation" that is presumably inherent in their "nationalism." The only one who has tackled the hardest question—the problem of the land—has been Eldridge Cleaver. He once tried to deal directly with "The Land Question and Black Liberation." At one point he came close to what the trouble has been: "Thus, it is not surprising that the average black man in America is schizoid on the question of his relationship to the nation as a whole, and there is a side of him that feels only the vaguest, most halting, tentative and even fleeting kinship with America. The feeling of alienation and dissociation is real and black people long ago would have readily identified themselves with another sovereignty had a viable one existed." Cleaver then went on to argue that no viable alternative sovereignty had ever existed. He had high praise for Marcus Garvey, but it turned out that Garvey "did not solve the specific question of Afro-America and its immediate relationship to the land beneath her feet. The practical prospect of Garvey's actual transporting blacks back to Africa turned most black people off because of a world situation and balance of power that made such a situation impossible." He gave Elijah Muhammad credit for knowing "that he had to deal with Afro-America's land hunger." And Cleaver considered Muhammad tactically wise enough to be "very careful never to identify any specific geographical location when he issued his call for land for Afro-America." Stokely Carmichael's thesis of Black Power, Cleaver said, "does not attempt to answer the land question. It does not deny the existence of that question, but rather frankly states that at the present moment the land question cannot be dealt with, that black people must put first things first, that there are a few things that must be done before we can deal with the land question."

Yet Cleaver went on to insist: "The necessity upon Afro-America is to move, now, to begin functioning as a nation, to assume its sovereignty, to demand that that sovereignty be recognized by other nations of the world." But where? The closest Cleaver came to meeting the issue was:

> Black Power must be viewed as a projection of sovereignty, an embryonic sovereignty that black people can focus on and through which they can make distinctions between themselves and others, between themselves and their enemies—in short, between the white mother country of America and the black colony dispersed throughout the continent on absentee-owned land, making Afro-America a decentralized colony. Black Power says to black people that it is possible for them to build a national organization on somebody else's land.

What is "sovereignty" without land to be sovereign of? How project "sovereignty" on "somebody else's land"? What is a "decentralized colony"? Is it made up of black ghettos in New York, Chicago, Oakland, and elsewhere, separated from one another by hundreds of miles? Is ghetto "sovereignty" a truly embryonic form of national sovereignty? It may be possible to build a national organization on somebody else's land, but how build a nation on that land?

Cleaver did not raise these questions, but he was not unaware that his notion of "embryonic sovereignty" might need some clarification. He therefore seized on what he considered to be the "parallel" between early Zionism and present-day black nationalism. The Jews, he pointed out, had also been cooped up in East European ghettos. Argentina and Uganda were considered as possible sites for a Jewish homeland before the decision was finally made in favor of Palestine. The Zionists founded a virtual government-in-exile for a people in exile. Cleaver concluded: "They would build their organization, their government, and then later on they would get some land and set the government and the people down on the land, like placing one's hat on top of one's head. The Jews did it. It worked. So now Afro-Americans must do the same thing." [28]

Cleaver could hardly have chosen a more unfortunate "parallel" for his cause. It is entirely based on the circumstance that the Jewish Zionists in the beginning did not have a national territorial base and were not even sure where it would be. But of one thing the Jewish Zionists were always sure—that they could not set up a national homeland in their East European ghettos. If black nationalism in the United States were prepared to get out of the American ghettos and set up a nation in Africa or elsewhere, the Zionist "parallel" might be helpful, though here again historical differences might dictate against pushing it too far. Black nationalist "Zionism" inevitably heads toward a Back-to-Africa conclusion, which Cleaver and the Black Panthers reject. The "parallel" begins promisingly but ends disastrously.

In an interview with *Playboy* (October 1968) Cleaver was questioned about the plan adopted by a National Black Government Conference, which met in Detroit in April 1968, for a "Republic of New Africa" to be made up of five Southern states. "Do you think that's a viable plan?" Cleaver was asked. "I don't have any sympathy with that approach," Cleaver replied, "but the Black Panthers feel that it's a proposal black people should be polled on." [29] From Cleaver's articles and the interview, it is hard to see just what kind of viable approach he would sympathize with.

In some ways the Panthers have inherited the ambiguous legacy of Malcolm X. Like him, they have moved in the direction of a social rather than a purely nationalist revolution. By adding socialism to nationalism, they had to broaden their horizons to make room for whites as well as blacks, if not in their own organizations, then in some form of "alliance" and "coalition." The Panthers' position has opened them up to attacks on two sides—from those who want a black nationalism not dependent for its ultimate success on a white social revolution, and those who want a social revolution untainted by black nationalism. It has not been easy for them to maintain their uneasy equilibrium between these two camps.

Black Power

8

The Black Panthers have not been the only ones to have trouble with the notion of a "black colony" in the United States. It had already figured prominently in the thinking of others, including Stokely Carmichael, who first popularized the slogan "Black Power." Carmichael's political pilgrimage in a single decade from a new form of the internal struggle for power to a new form of emigrationism showed how much the new and the old were mixed together in the latest phase of black nationalism in America.

In April 1960, the Student Nonviolent Coordinating Committee (SNCC) was formed in Raleigh, North Carolina. It was an outgrowth of a student sit-in campaign, itself the outgrowth of the movement set in motion five years earlier by the victorious bus boycott in Montgomery, Alabama, led by Dr. Martin Luther King, Jr. In 1961, Carmichael, born in Trinidad but educated in the United States, then only twenty years old and a student at Howard University, was arrested in Jackson, Mississippi, and came out of jail a full-time SNCC organizer. SNCC's staff grew from two in 1960 to 200 full-time paid workers plus 250 full-time volunteers in 1965.[1] In this period, SNCC was made up of both whites and blacks, and they devoted most of their energies to a voter-registration campaign. Their most ambitious undertaking was the Mississippi Freedom Democratic Party, which made an unsuccessful bid for official recognition at the national convention of the Democratic Party at Atlantic City, New Jersey, in August 1964. The disappointment led the following year to the building of the Lowndes County Freedom Organization in Alabama, the word "Democratic" significantly dropped as a token of rejection of the existing party system. Besides Carmichael, James Forman, Julian Bond, H. Rap Brown, and others have graduated from the SNCC school of politics.

In 1966 the new chairman of SNCC, Carmichael, made it an all-black organization. That summer, during a march in Mississippi, he came to be identified with the phrase, "Black Power," that seemed to sum up the mood of the moment. As he first used it, the sense seemed to be both anti-integrationist and anti-separatist. He demanded, in effect, that American blacks should organize themselves independently of whites, as they had done in SNCC, "in order to speak from a position of strength" in American political, social, and economic life. "We have to move to control the economics and politics of our community so the southside [in Chicago] cannot be controlled by a [Mayor] Daley," he held.[2] He denied that the slogan could be equated with "racism or separatism," and he tried to envisage what might happen in Lowndes County, where 80 per cent of the population was black, to explain the meaning of the term:

> In Lowndes County, for example, black power will mean that if a Negro is elected sheriff, he can end police brutality. If a black man is elected tax assessor, he can collect

and channel funds for the building of better roads and schools serving black people—thus advancing the move from political power into the economic arena. In such areas as Lowndes, where black men have a majority, they will attempt to use it to exercise control. This is what they seek: control. Where Negroes lack a majority, black power means proper representation and sharing of control. It means the creation of power bases from which black people can work to change statewide or nationwide patterns of oppression through pressure from strength—instead of weakness.[3]

This objective was still well within the bounds of—and even presupposed—the existing American nation. Carmichael also looked forward to an eventual coalition between poor blacks and poor whites based on "the cooperative concept in business and banking." At the same time, however, he referred to the black ghettos as "colonies of the United States" which "must be liberated." [4] But this allusion was never thought through at this time, though it held the seeds of his future political development.

In 1967 this hitherto minor intimation became the momentous major premise of the book *Black Power,* by Carmichael and Charles V. Hamilton. This work evidently reflected the thinking, as far as Carmichael was concerned, of a previous period—or as much as he thought it prudent to make public. But the book has lived a life of its own and deserves to be considered on its own terms.

According to Carmichael and Hamilton, "black people in this country form a colony." This colony, they hastily admit, is no ordinary, recognizable one. In order to make "colonialism" fit American conditions, they quickly redefine it as but another name for "institutional racism." In the next sentence they recognize a difficulty: "Obviously, the analogy is not perfect." The first reason for its imperfection, as they see it, takes us close to our main concern:

One normally associates a colony with a land and people

subjected to, and physically separated from, the "Mother Country." This is not always the case, however; in South Africa and Rhodesia, black and white inhabit the same land —with blacks subordinated to whites just as in the English, French, Italian, Portuguese, and Spanish colonies. It is the objective relationship which counts, not rhetoric (such as constitutions articulating equal rights) or geography.[5]

It is, of course, true that blacks and whites inhabit the same land in South Africa and Rhodesia—about four blacks to one white in the Union of South Africa and about seventeen blacks to one white in Rhodesia. In the United States the proportion is approximately one black to nine whites. In addition, South Africa and Rhodesia were black lands before they were colonized by whites only in the last century. Whites and blacks came to the United States in very different circumstances. To cite South Africa and Rhodesia as colonial prototypes for the United States because whites and blacks inhabit the same land in all three obviously leaves much to be desired.

We are confronted here with a simple confusion of terms. A colony requires something more than political, economic, and social discrimination or oppression, especially of a minority. It requires precisely what Carmichael and Hamilton deny—a historic relationship of a people to a land. Without this relationship, there may be discrimination or oppression, but not the status of a colony.*

If Black America really constituted a colony, the implications would be relatively simple and obvious. Colonies rebel to throw out their alien rulers and establish national independence and sovereignty. The Algerians rose against the French, expelled them *en masse,* and set up their own state.

---

* The Carmichael-Hamilton redefinition of "colonialism" resembles Huey Newton's later effort to equate it with "exploitation." What seems to be happening is that "colonialism" is becoming an all-purpose word for social and political evils. If this trend continues, the term is going to mean so many different things that it will become less and less meaningful.

If American blacks truly constituted a colony, Carmichael and Hamilton would no doubt have advocated the same course in the United States. That they did not, that they in fact advocated something much less and very different in the name of Black Power indicated that they were misusing their key term.

For when Carmichael and Hamilton spelled out their own program, what did they propose? In the main, they wanted blacks, as they put it, to "close ranks," to gain control of their own communities, to obtain "black self-determination and black self-identity." But for what purpose? They said that the black ethnic group must first close ranks in order to "enter the open society." They called for power bases, of strength, "from which black people can press to change local or nationwide patterns of oppression—instead of from weakness." Their ultimate values and goals were, they insisted, "an effective share in the total power of the society." Black self-determination and black self-identity—by which they meant Black Power—aimed at "full participation in the decision-making processes affecting the lives of black people, and recognition of the virtues in themselves as black people." Indeed, they summed up their goal in terms that fair-minded and decent whites could easily accept: "Ultimately, the gains of our struggle will be meaningful only when consolidated by viable coalitions between blacks and whites who accept each other as co-equal partners and who identify their goals as politically and economically similar. At this stage, given the nature of the society, distinct roles must be played." [6]

But where did all this leave the concept of an existing black "colony" within the United States? It could not possibly mean what the Algerians meant in relation to the French. The "colony" that Carmichael and Hamilton claimed to represent did not aim at nationhood; at no point did they even refer to nationhood. They wanted little more than a fair share of the historic American commitment. They decried the rhetoric of equal constitutional rights but were not above the rhetoric of a colonial revolution that was neither truly colonial nor truly revolutionary. A true colony in revolt aims at more than full participation in the decision-making process of the existing nation; a true revolution aims at overthrowing the existing decision-making process, not at participating in it.

By 1967, however, Carmichael for one had gone far beyond the position set forth in this book. In July of that year he made a speech in London in which he redefined Black Power in international rather than in American terms. By this time he had come to identify poor American blacks not with poor American whites but with people of the so-called Third World, with whom they shared a common colonial status. He reinterpreted Marx to include the American working class among the beneficiaries of capitalist exploitation, and advanced a new—if hardly original—formula: "The proletariat has become the Third World, and the bourgeoisie is white western society." And he redefined his key term: "Black Power, to us, means that black people see themselves as part of a new force, sometimes called the Third World; that we see our struggle as closely related to liberation struggles around the world." In the book, Carmichael had written as if Black Power sought to win a position of strength for black Americans in the United States; in this speech, he made Black Power stand for a virtual declaration of war against the United States.[7]

After Carmichael's strange interlude with the Black Panthers in 1968, he abandoned the United States altogether. In January 1969, Carmichael went abroad to join the deposed President of Ghana, Dr. Kwame Nkrumah, in exile in nearby Guinea. After his split with the Panthers, Carmichael frankly explained: "I know that I cannot provide the leadership right now in America. I do not know how to begin to cope with the problems, so for me to stay there and to pretend that I do is for me to deceive myself and my people." [8] This sense of failure and helplessness drove Carmichael to adopt a position more than faintly reminiscent of the nineteenth-century emigrationists.

He came to believe, he said, that "one of the most important things we must now begin to do, is to call ourselves 'African.' No matter where we may be from, we are first of all and finally Africans. Africans. Africans. Africans." As for white Americans, they were something else, too: "America, in fact, is nothing but Europe. The white people in America are not Americans but in fact Europeans." He, therefore, had concluded that "the solution has to be Pan-Africanism." Even for black Americans (or, as he preferred to put it, "Africans who live in America"), he did not think that "in the States there can be a clear and viable alternative for black people." It was especially necessary to make them understand that their real culture was African and that they had to alienate themselves "from the culture and values of Western society." But Pan-Africanism, as he saw it, needed a "land base" from which to fight for the unification of Africa and to fight against "all of Europe." That base was Ghana, and the leader whom Carmichael had been waiting for and seeking was Dr. Nkrumah. What Ghana, with a population of little more than eight million, could mean in the immediate future as a "land base" for over three times as many black people in America was not made altogether clear. The idea seemed to be that any real progress in America had to wait for the restoration of Dr. Nkrumah to power in Ghana and the unification of Africa by a Nkrumah-led Ghana.[9]

To some extent, Carmichael's hopes for Ghana in 1969 curiously resembled those of Bishop Holly for Haiti one hundred and ten years earlier. This was Carmichael's second or third try at what Black Power was and how to get there, and it was not likely to be his last. Meanwhile, the once-flourishing SNCC had become virtually defunct.

There are others, too, who have had trouble with the notion of a black "colony" in the United States. It has become the fashionable cliché of present-day black nationalism, though few of those who use it quite know what to do with it. Those who use the terms "colony" and "nation" in connection with American Negroes should be obligated to tell us what the implications of those terms are. Is it a "nation" which is striving to be sovereign and independent on its own soil? Is it a "colony" which is striving to become a "nation"? Or is it a different kind of "colony" which cannot by force of circumstances become a nation? Is it a different kind of "nation" which does not have a national territory and cannot aspire to sovereignty and independence? One black nationalist has called on black intellectuals to "engage in nation-building through myth-making." [10] The trouble with this is that nations make myths but myths do not make nations.

Both the strength and weakness of the Black Power slogan may be traced to its ambiguity or at least its indefiniteness. It sprang from a nationalist urge without getting into any of the nationalist dilemmas. It avoided trouble by the simple expedient of leaving undefined what kind of "power" it had in mind. Black capitalists as well as black separatist revolutionaries could adopt it for very different purposes. In this way it satisfied almost everyone, and in the end, satisfied no one fully. As a slogan it was an outstanding success; as a policy it left all the hard questions—questions.

Another evangelist of Black Power, Julius Lester, informed his readers that "blacks are a colonial people within" the United States. Black power was preparing for the "day of reckoning." He went on: "The concept of the black man as a nation, which is only being talked about now, will become reality when violence comes. Out of the violence will come the new nation (if the violence is successful) and the new man." What made him so sure that the black man in America constituted a nation? "We are a distinct cultural group, proud of our culture and our institutions, and simply want to be left alone to lead our good, black lives." [11] That was as close as he came to defining the nature of this nation.

Lester's version was one way to get around the troublesome "land question" by, in effect, ignoring or bypassing it. This strategy has been adopted by those who base black nationalism on "culture" or "consciousness" without attempting to attach it to any particular national territory. This approach tends to assume or to allege that there is something culturally unique about the American Negro, as if this were equivalent to a recognizable national existence.

It is not easy, however, to define what is culturally unique in the American Negro. Lester's effort is typical of one approach. "The uniqueness of black culture can be explained," he ventures, "in that it is a culture whose emphasis is on the nonverbal, i.e., the nonconceptual." In black culture, "it is the experience that counts, not what is said." And further: "The black man knows the inherent irrationality of life." How this nonverbal, nonconceptual "culture" operates is illustrated by Lester as follows: "When the black preacher shouts, 'God is a living God!' don't argue. Get ready to shake hands with the Lord Almighty. 'I talked to God this morning and I said, "Now, listen here, Lord. You got to do something about these white folks down here. Lord, they giving us a hard time. You got to do something!" ' God is like a personal friend, an old buddy, whom you talk to man-to-man." [12]

It is remarkable how similar this stereotype is to Thomas Jefferson's classical stereotype of Negro inferiority. Jefferson thought that Negroes were more capable of "sensation than reflection." He found them "in reason much inferior." He was prepared to agree that they were "more ardent," more generally gifted musically, and not inferior morally, but he drew the line at—to use Lester's term—their ability to conceptualize. The abiding influence of Jefferson's views on the Negroes' alleged mental inferiority has been emphasized by Professor Winthrop D. Jordan in his massive work *White Over Black*. Yet the key idea has now come back in the guise of attributing to it the function of creating a unique culture. One wonders whether Lester's latest black stereotype should not be just as offensive, at least to Negro intellectuals, as Jefferson's antiquated black stereotype, and whether the former would not in the long run produce just as much harm. In any case, "a colonial people" is essentially a political, not a cultural, conception, and it is hard to see how cultural nationalists like Lester can get very far without a minimum of such conceptualization.

A different and somewhat more subtle effort was once made by LeRoi Jones, the black poet and playwright. He raised the question of what was authentically Negroid about American Negro literature, but his views took in the whole range of Negro artistic and cultural expression. Jones argued that Negro literature and art had been, with rare exceptions, "of an almost agonizing mediocrity." He attributed this failure to the desire of Negro intellectuals to prove how "cultivated" they were by white standards. Music, he maintained, was the one exception to the rule. In blues, jazz, and spirituals, he saw the persistence of African influences that had been eradicated everywhere else. But he insisted that American Negro music was not an African art; it was, rather, "a fusion between African musical tradition and the American experience"; it was, in fact, an American art. "Africanisms do exist in Negro culture," he contended, "but they have been so translated and transmuted by the American experience that they have become integral parts of that experience." And he explained: "The paradox of the Negro experience in America is that it is a separate experience, but inseparable from the complete fabric of American life." [13]

This analysis implies that there is something uniquely Negroid in Negro music, but that it is not an independent, self-sufficient phenomenon. A mixture of African elements and American experience was necessary to produce this cultural expression, which, if we may trust Jones, could not be reproduced in the other arts because the African elements have been missing. If so, the difficulty has been that such a mixture cannot be arranged artificially or arbitrarily. In the case of music, it had old and deep historical roots that permitted it to have a continuous historical development from the earliest period of the Negro in America. But can African culture be injected into the American experience in Negro literature and the other arts at this late date? Can black nationalism take the place of African cultural elements to produce a similarly unique and original fusion? Jones's insights into Negro music do not transfer very easily to the other expressions of Negro culture.*

Not only is the uniqueness of American Negro culture difficult to define but, wherever and whatever it is, it is still, as Jones persuasively put it, "inseparable from the complete fabric of American life." In any event, culture should not be equated with nation; culture is a far less clearly defined and localized concept than nation. There can be a distinct culture without an independent nation, and an independent nation without a distinct culture. The Algerians, for example, did not have to stress their cultural difference from the French; they knew that they were a different people who inhabited a different land; Frantz Fanon was deeply French in his culture and yet fanatically pro-Algerian in his nationalism (though he was born in Martinique). That there were cultural differences undoubtedly reinforced the Algerian national consciousness, but Algeria did not owe its nationhood to these cultural differences.

* This essay was written by Jones in 1962. More recently a white art historian, Professor Robert Farris Thompson, has argued that African influences in wood sculpture, basketry, and ceramics persisted in the deep South. But most of his examples come from the nineteenth century and even then seem rather limited in quantity and scope ("African Influence on the Art of the United States," in Black Studies in the University [New Haven, Conn.: Yale University Press, 1969], pp. 122–70). In any case, LeRoi Jones was thinking of art forms or cultural expressions which had reached a much higher level, though it may be necessary to revise the older view that African culture in all but music had been completely "eradicated."

The problem, in fact, is not so much lack of conceptualization, as Julius Lester wants to believe, as the wrong kind. Harold Cruse has rightly cautioned that "if the Negro leadership is hampered by deficient conceptualizing of American group reality, then the Negro movement will defeat itself in the long run." [14] His critique of Negro intellectuals, which is really a critique of what he calls "Afro-American nationalism," has the great merit of manifestly coming from an independent, critical mind, whatever shortcomings it may have.

Cruse once drops a hint that the American Negro has been the subject of "a special kind of North American domestic colonialism"—but he never follows it up. He touches on the "land question" with a remark that it "can be solved only from an urban base of political power." He adds for good measure the provocative thought that the American "land question" is now "an international issue involving Africa," which leads him to put forth the extraordinary suggestion that "there may well come a time when the race question in Africa will have to be solved by admitting specified numbers of white Rhodesians, Angolans, and South African Afrikaaners into the United States, in exchange for an equal number of Afro-Americans to take their places in Africa." [15] What such an exchange would involve or in what possible circumstances it might take place he leaves totally unanswered—and unasked.

To the extent that one can make out Cruse's own position, which is never developed systematically, it has little to do with "domestic colonialism" or the "land question." Cruse's main positive contribution—when he can tear himself away from paying back old scores against other Negro intellectuals—hinges on the *ethnic,* rather than the racial, character of the American Negro problem (his italics).[16] He chases other leads fitfully and sporadically, but he has most to say, and most originally, about the ethnic factor. Thus Cruse is at his best when he acutely distinguishes between "having a nationalistic mood and having nationalist objectives in politics, economics, and culture that relate to how Negroes as a people exist in America." [17] The mood is real enough, but history and circumstance may preclude it from relating realistically to the condition in which the American Negro finds himself. Such a conflict is likely to produce political fantasy: "The American Negro is wedded to America and does not want to return to his ancestral Africa except in fancy, perhaps." Even Africans may suffer from this duality: "The African has Africa, but a severe psychic problem has cropped up among Africans sent to the United States on various assignments: Many of them feel alienated within themselves, but do not want to return to Africa. Alienated or no, they have become passionately attached to the ways of the cosmopolitan West, the high standard of living, the creature comforts of the affluent society." [18]

As Cruse sees it, "the problem [of the American Negro] will be solved under specifically American conditions or it will never be solved, for Afro-American Nationalism is basically a black reflection of the unsolved American nationality question." By "nationality," Cruse evidently means what the dictionary defines as "an ethnic group constituting one element of a larger unit (as a nation)." This nationality—not national—question, he says, involves several ethnic groups, not Negroes alone. But two are crucial—"Anglo-Saxon Protestants and American Negroes." In between them he sees another major group, the Jews, who make up the third component of his "fateful triangle." Cruse's chief grievance against the Jews seems to be that they have come between the Anglo-Saxon Protestants and the Negroes; he is most wrathful against Jewish Communists for having acted out "the role of political surrogates for the 'white' working class, and thereby gained the political whip of intellectual and theoretical domination of the Negro question." [19] The Communists, and especially the Jewish Communists, obsess Cruse to such an extent that he devotes far too much of his book to them, sometimes in a manner bordering on the absurd.* In general, his idea seems to be that the Negroes must solve the American nationality problem by making a direct deal with the "Anglo-Saxons" without the intervention of the Jews who, he hints, have ideologically dominated the Negroes.[20] Whatever merit there may be in this view, it takes us a long way from the perspective of black nationhood. In the end, Cruse advises the Negro intellectual that his "special function" is cultural.[21] Yet "cultural nationalism" by itself implies or requires little more than the status of an ethnic minority. Unless "cultural nationalism" is hinged to some form of separate nationhood, in or out of the present United States, it need never get beyond the ethnic status.

One of the few things Carmichael and Hamilton, Lester, and Cruse have in common is a mutual antipathy for "integrationism" and "integrationists." Otherwise, they and all the other tendencies demonstrate that black nationalism today is not a party and has no party line—or it has too many parties and too many party lines. It can be identified more easily by what it is against than by what it is for. It is still seeking the right answers, but it is not yet clear that it has been asking all the right questions.

---

* "Under Jewish Communist prodding, the [American] Communist Party took up the anti-Hitler crusade in the late 1930's," Cruse wrote (*The Crisis of the Negro Intellectual*, p. 168). The "crusade" was, of course, taken up in the early 1930s. There is something ludicrous about the notion that it was "Jewish Communist prodding," not Soviet Communist prodding, that turned American Communists into anti-Hitler crusaders. Cruse refers to the "Jewish crusade on the Left against Hitler" as if there would have been no crusade without the Jews, and as if anti-Hitlerism were a specific Jewish creation.

The Land Question

9

In the early 1960s most of the black nationalist movements active in the United States, mainly in Harlem, were still oriented toward Africa. In addition to the Nation of Islam, there was a rival Muslim group, the Muslim Brotherhood, which claimed to possess a monopoly of true Muslimism. The United African Nationalist Movement had been founded in 1948 by James R. Lawson, a former official of the Harlem Labor Union. The Universal African Nationalist Movement, headed by Benjamin Gibbons, looked upon itself as the orthodox heir of Garvey's UNIA. The African Nationalist Pioneer Movement was another Garveyite splinter group. A Cultural Association for Women of African Heritage, a Liberation Committee for Africa, an On Guard Committee for Freedom, and a Provisional Committee for a Free Africa also held forth.

"We must Africanize everything!" proclaimed

Priest Reverend Ofuntola Oserjeman Adefunmi of the Yoruba Temple of New Oyo, which was the new African name for Harlem. His message suggested a short cut to Africanization: "Note to men: adopt the African look; cut the brim off your hats, you will look like you should, and less like an imitation. Change!" In 1961 the Priest Reverend also founded the New Alajo Party as an African-oriented political movement. Its manifesto announced: "The re-Africanization of the black people of America has begun. Like yeast in a hot oven we are suddenly beginning to rise. Each person must do his part." One demand of the party was "millions of dollars in indemnity for slavery." [1]

By 1963 a shift in direction was noticeable. The Alajo Party, also known as the African Nationalist Independence-Partition Party of North America, formed a "Provisional Government of the African-American Captive Nation," which issued a "Declaration of Self-Determination of the African-American Captive Nation" in January 1963. The Declaration proposed that the United States of America show its magnanimity as well as greatness by agreeing that "all land south of the Mason-Dixon line where our people constitute the majority, be partitioned to establish a territory for Self-Government for the African Nation in the United States." It also suggested that the United States government "take full responsibility for training our people for self-government in all its ramifications" and immediately recognize the Provisional Government of the African-American Captive Nation. A well-informed observer estimated that there were more than two dozen Afro-American "nationalist" organizations in Harlem at this time—with a combined membership of 5000 out of a total population of about 600,000.[2]

In the following year Malcolm X broke with the Muslims and went off to struggle with the great questions of black destiny alone. For the most part, however, Malcolm still represented a strong African orientation, especially to those who could not follow every detail of his swiftly changing views. Nevertheless, a change was on the way. In 1963–64 the Student Nonviolent Coordinating Committee, then in its heyday of black-and-white "integration," sponsored a voter-registration and community-organizing drive in Mississippi. The historic march from Selma to Montgomery, Alabama, led by Martin Luther King, Jr., took place in March 1965 and led to the passage of the Voting Rights Bill. The crest of both the "integrationist" and Back-to-Africa waves came in the mid-1960s, after which they gave way to a militantly nationalist, separatist but non-African phase.

As one participant in the next wave explained, most American Negroes who went to Africa after World War II discovered that they could not feel at home in the newly independent countries, which they had thought of as their homeland. "If we have been separated from Africa for so long that we are no longer quite at ease there," he concluded, "then we are left with only one place to make our home, and that is the land to which we were brought in chains." [3] By the late 1960s the Back-to-Africa tendency had been reduced to little more than superficial "cultural" manifestations, such as hairdos and fashions. Territorially, the most extreme wing of black nationalism, which would be satisfied with nothing less than a clearly defined nation, had swung over to locating it in the United States.

One of those who went from the "integrationist" wave to the separatist wave was LeRoi Jones. In 1965, in an essay entitled "The Legacy of Malcolm X, and the Coming of the Black Nation," Jones noted that most black nationalist movements in the United States still advocated some form of Back-to-Africa-ism or preferred to leave the "land question" alone. He attributed the shift away from Garvey's pro-Africa influence to the tendency of Elijah Muhammad's Muslims to identify themselves with the land "where they lived." Then came Malcolm X, whose greatest contributions, Jones thought, were awakening a Black National consciousness and tying it up with the so-called Third World.

As we have seen, as long as Malcolm X was still a Muslim, he emphasized that land was primary in any nationalism or revolution and he could conceive of land for black Americans only in Africa. After breaking with the Muslims, he increasingly questioned this view and ended by repudiating the whole notion of a "black state" even in America and by giving up the very expression "black nationalism."

Nevertheless, LeRoi Jones still chose to evoke the Malcolm X who, he told the reader, "said many times that when you speak about revolution you're talking about land"—which was true but not the whole truth. Thus covered by the mantle of Malcolm X, Jones proceeded to advance his own view of the "land" question. Jones went the whole way: "We do not want a Nation, we are a Nation." And a nation meant land: "We begin by being Nationalists. But a nation is land, and wars are fought over land." This point was stressed again and again: "It is impossible to be a Nationalist without talking about land."

Where was Jones's "land"? He had a ready and blithely simple answer: "What the Black Man must do now is look down at the ground upon which he stands, and claim it as his own. It is not abstract. Look down! Pick up the earth, or jab your fingernails into the concrete. It is real and it is yours, if you want it." Jones himself set the example: "In Harlem, for instance, as director of the Black Arts Repertory Theatre School, I have issued a call for a Black Nation. In Harlem, where 600,000 Black People reside." He also called for the nationalization of all white property in this Black Nation; the elimination of all white politicians as well as "Black politicians doing funny servant business for whites"; and the power to make "treaties, agreements, laws." [4]

Thus, in the name of a Malcolm X who had just repudiated a black nation anywhere in North America, LeRoi Jones came out for a Black Nation in Harlem. In 1967 he went somewhat further. In another essay he sought to cope with the problem of "space." Black Power, he said, already controlled black enclaves and cities, but that was not enough. "Further control must be nationalization, separation." And this in turn, he went on, signified "absolute control of resources beneficial to a national group." [5] At this point Jones consciously or accidentally touched on a real problem. What and how much would it take to give Harlem, Hough, or Watts "absolute control" of the resources—let us say, the jobs—necessary to make their nationalization and separation viable? But such considerations had no attraction for Jones, who is, after all, only a part-time political thinker. Nor is he the only one who seems to think that every black ghetto and enclave should promote itself to the status of a Black Nation. In 1969, a writer in a black nationalist organ referred to the "enclaves of Black Power like Lowndes County" and the "Black Power bases in the Northern ghettos" as "Black Nations." [6] The plural suggests how confused and confusing the terminology has become.

This was one answer to the "land question." Others were more expansive.

A major effort to arrive at a black nationalist program took place at the Conference on Black Power which met in Newark, New Jersey, in July 1967. One of its high points was a resolution presented by Professor Robert S. Browne, assistant professor of economics at Fairleigh Dickinson University, which called for initiating "a national dialogue on the desirability of partitioning the United States into two separate and independent nations, one to be a homeland for white and the other to be a homeland for black Americans." This proposal received a thunderous ovation, though Browne later admitted that all those who voted for it could "by no stretch of the imagination be considered active partisans of the idea of a separate state." Evidently it was the kind of proposal that some, perhaps many, Negroes would applaud without necessarily wanting to do anything about.

Professor Browne represented the soft-sell approach to "The Case for Black Separatism," as one of his articles, widely circulated in black nationalist study circles, was entitled. He insisted that the Newark resolution did not try to prejudge the merits of the proposal; it merely asked that "the legal, political, economic, and sociological implications" of the partition be seriously discussed and examined. He even presented the case as if it came from the "moderate center" and warned that failure to take it seriously would sentence the country to the "terror" of irresponsible extremists. He offered the division of British India into today's India and Pakistan as the precedent for what he had in mind. For the most part he contented himself with getting both whites and blacks accustomed to the idea of partition. His message was that "a sense of nationhood is groping for expression" in the black ghettos, and it may lead to two separate nations or to "some as yet untried type of human community." In another article, in the *New York Times Magazine* of August 11, 1968, in which he largely repeated himself, Professor Browne based his separatist argument solely on the difference in the American Negroes' ethnic culture.

The hard-sell approach has been represented by the National Black Government Conference, which met in Detroit in April 1968 (with which Cleaver was not sympathetic). It immediately set up a Republic of New Africa, to be made up of five Southern states—Louisiana, Mississippi, Alabama, Georgia, and South Carolina. It endowed this Republic of New Africa with a self-chosen government headed by Robert F. Williams, a fugitive from 1961 to 1969 in Cuba, China, and elsewhere, as President;* a Michigan lawyer, Milton R. Henry, as First Vice-President; a Second Vice-President, Treasurer, and Ministers of Justice, Interior, Finance, Culture and Education, and Defense. It also has a military arm, the Black Legion, whose members wear black uniforms with

* Upon his return to the United States, Mr. Williams resigned from this post in December 1969.

leopard-skin epaulettes, black berets, black combat boots with white laces, and white pistol belts, without weapons. At a "legislative conference" held in Washington, D.C., in August 1969, many delegates wore African garb and head-dresses. An observer noted that most delegates were youthful and "primarily from the urban North." [7] Thus the organization reflected the peculiar contradiction of urban Northerners costumed as Africans demanding a Republic of New Africa in the more rural Southern states where they themselves did not live.

According to Robert Sherrill, who published a lengthy interview with First Vice-President Henry, who also called himself "Brother Gaidi," this Michigan lawyer was the real headman of this outfit. Logically, Henry said, the black population should go back to Africa, "but logistically it is very unsound because of the difficulties of moving people, furniture, mastering the culture." However, one African custom—polygamy—would be reinstated. He also envisaged a dictatorship of the founders for the first thirty to forty years and the prohibition of all trade unions. To take over the five Southern states, Henry worked out a strategy that consisted of gaining control of them, county by county, starting with Mississippi, which had the largest percentage of blacks. Economically, this entailed buying up land, as the Jews bought land in Palestine, for which purpose "Malcolm X land certificates" were offered for sale at the price of $100 each. Politically, Henry saw control of the sheriffs' offices as the key to control of the land. "Then we will have a legitimate military force, legitimate under U.S. law, made up of people who can be deputized and armed."

Henry was asked if they could whip the United States Army. "With the aid of nuclear weapons from our allies, such as China, sure we could," he replied. "China would never help us until we could show that we were capable of a separate, independent existence. But we could show that by controlling a land mass." And if Chinese nuclear power was not enough? He had another weapon: "We've got second-strike power right now in our guerrillas within the metropolitan areas—black men, armed. Say we start taking over Mississippi—which we are capable of doing right now—and the United States started to interfere. Well, our guerrillas all over the country would strike." [8]

It may be hard to take this kind of tall talk seriously. The Republic of New Africa has done little to make good its threat in the South, but at least one separatist action that it has sponsored took place in the North on a much smaller scale. In March 1969 it injected itself into the Ocean Hill-Brownsville strife in Brooklyn, New York, with an "independence project" to separate the "beleaguered community of Ocean Hill–Brownsville from the United States." The Minister of Interior, Brother Imari,* announced a "vote" to take the neighborhood "outside the U.S. Federal system, and as part of the Republic of New Africa." [9] This project was put in charge of the Minister of Education, Herman Ferguson, a former assistant principal in a public school in the borough of Queens, who was reported appealing a seven-year sentence for having conspired to murder Roy Wilkins, executive director of the NAACP, and Whitney Young, executive director of the National Urban League. Ferguson claimed that 1047 community residents, or 13 per cent of all those over the age of sixteen, had taken part in the vote, and he held out the prospect of a future plebiscite in which "voters will be asked to give their consent to be separated from the U.S. Government and ask us to govern them." [10] Oddly enough, Vice-President Henry had previously assured Robert Sherrill that he disapproved of independent black cities because "the whites would have us surrounded." [11]

---

* "Brother Imari" was Richard Henry, brother of First Vice-President Milton Henry. The two brothers split in January 1970, when Milton refused to attend a conference dominated by Richard. Milton Henry declared that "those who want to live under an idiotic dictatorship are welcome to leave with Imari" (*The New York Times*, January 27, 1970).

Another version of the takeover has been put forward by Floyd McKissick, former national director of the Congress of Racial Equality (CORE). McKissick also maintained: "Black people in the United States live in a state of *de facto* nationhood." All they lack, he claimed, is independence. To enable the black people to make use of the present electoral system, the federal government has to make it possible for more black sheriffs and black tax collectors to be elected in counties with a black majority. This development would cause whites to move out in large numbers, and open the way for blacks to move in. McKissick foresaw black control of two or three states in a single generation. For some reason, however, in the end he stopped short of ushering in a new stage of independent nationhood for the black-controlled states. His conclusion seemed somewhat anticlimactic: "When Black People are in control of at least a few American states, they will be able to exert enough influence within the federal system to affect the treatment of their Black brothers in America's urban centers, as well as the exercise of American foreign policy." [12] It is hard to see why the black people in the United States need to be a *de facto* nation to exert this kind of influence.

A three-phase plan—"short-range," "mid-range," and "long-range"—has been concocted by Roy Innis, present national director of CORE. Phase I is based on a Community Self-Determination Bill to enable blacks to take over the economy of black communities through federally supported credit and underwriting. Phase II calls for black control of all other institutions in black communities, including schools, police, government, hospitals, and the like. Phase III contemplates the drafting of a new United States constitution, because, it is said, "when America's blacks cease to relate to the larger nation as a dependent and colonized people and begin to assert power through the control of their community institutions and capital instruments, the black 'colony' will then in fact be a 'nation within a nation.' " The final phase is frankly "separatist" in outlook, and the new constitution would presumably give formal, legal expression to a two-nation set-up, whatever form it might take in practice.[13]

All these plans have one curious characteristic. They serve notice in advance that they want and need the good offices of the present federal government in order to make the black population independent of that government. More black sheriffs and black tax collectors, more federally supported credit and underwriting for black businesses, may very well be necessary and desirable, especially in predominantly black communities. But if anything is likely to stand in their way, it is loose thinking and writing about black "nationhood" and "separatism." For these terms imply that the federal government is expected to aid and abet the disruption and dissolution of the existing American nation. Such a strategy may seem clever to its proponents, but the likelihood of its being clever enough to work would seem to be very slight.

Paradoxically, this nationalist exuberance depends for whatever persuasiveness it may have on the relative success of the 1965 Voting Rights Act and the voter registration campaign. Black voter registration in Mississippi went up from 8 per cent in 1965 to 59 per cent by late 1968. Only this unprecedented increase enabled Charles Evers to defeat a white incumbent in the election for Mayor of Fayette, Mississippi, and permitted a black slate to score a victory in Greene County, Alabama, both in 1969. The number of black elected officials in the Southern states increased from seventy-two in 1965 to four hundred sixty-one in 1969. We may expect more, if it means, as Mayor Evers put it, making government "work for everybody," black and white alike. The gravest danger to this democratic achievement, overdue for a century, will come not only from die-hard white supremacists but from die-hard black nationalists. Both have a vested interest in exploiting the fantasy of a black takeover, municipality by municipality, county by county, state by state.

Professor Browne mentions the need for seriously considering "population relocation"; "Vice-President" Henry talks of setting up a Black Legion by arming sheriffs' deputies; Floyd McKissick foresees black control of counties leading to black control of states and beyond; Roy Innis looks forward to a new two-nation constitution. The magnitude of the problem, however, is never hinted at by them or by other black nationalists with similar ideas. According to the last census of 1960, the population in the five states chosen by the Republic of New Africa was divided as follows:

| | WHITE | | NON-WHITE | |
	Numbers	%	*Numbers*	%
Mississippi	1,257,546	58	915,743	42
South Carolina	1,551,022	65.2	829,291	34.8
Louisiana	2,211,715	68.1	1,039,207	31.9
Alabama	2,283,609	70	980,271	30
Georgia	2,817,223	71.5	1,122,596	28.5
Total	10,121,115	67.4	4,887,108	32.6

How much "population relocation" would be necessary in order to get a black population of 50 per cent in the five states? It would be necessary to move out one-half of the whites or move in an equal number of blacks. And these figures, formidable as they may be, imply nothing more than an equalization of the population, a balance that might be suitable for a biracial state. A black majority of even three-fourths—not too much to ask for a black state—would require the "relocation" of about two-thirds the present white population or moving in two or three times the number of blacks there now. And it should be remembered that the blacks have been moving in the opposite direction for half a century.

Another aspect of the problem deserves some attention.

Even in those states with the largest proportion of black population, the distribution of that population is highly significant. Mississippi is a case in point:

	URBAN	RURAL NONFARM	RURAL FARM
White	525,594	488,076	243,737
Non-White	295,211	326,421	299,102

These figures show that the black population is still largely concentrated in the rural areas. South Carolina is the only state in which, as in Mississippi, non-whites somewhat outnumber whites in the rural farm area. In all the other states, whites outnumber non-whites in all three categories. Thus, demographically, the whites are predominant, and decisively predominant, in or near the cities that control the main economic and political levers of power. "Population relocation" would be enormously complicated by this factor in the present balance of forces.

McKissick's theory of county control leading to state control may also be tested by a few figures. According to the 1960 census, the number of counties with white or black majorities in the five states is as follows:

	WHITE	BLACK
Mississippi	53	29
South Carolina	31	15
Georgia	125	34
Louisiana (parishes)	54	10
Alabama	56	11

Thus about a third of the counties in Mississippi and South Carolina have black majorities (some by a very narrow margin), a fifth in Georgia, and somewhat less in the other two states. Black majorities are concentrated in the most rural sectors. In Greene County, Alabama, blacks outnumber whites by more than three to one, but this is exceptional, and in no state could black political control of all the black-majority counties begin to take over the state.

Apart from all other considerations, what do these figures tell us about the allegedly "colonial" nature of the American Negro problem? In Algeria, for example, the proportion of Frenchmen to Algerians was unusually high for colonial rule. But even there, at the end of French rule, the French accounted for only 10 per cent of the total population. In the case of Pakistan, about 6.5 million Moslems moved into it from India and about 5.5 million Hindus moved out of it to India. But these numbers, huge as they were, must be measured against the total Pakistan population at that time of about 75 million. Algeria and Pakistan represented "population relocation" at its most extreme. Yet they cannot be compared with the problem posed by the five Southern states. In Algeria and Pakistan, the native populations rooted in the same land for centuries constituted the immense majority. A "colony" such as the black population in the Southern states is supposed to constitute, which consists of a minority and a shrinking one at that, presents an altogether different problem.

Whatever the best way to deal with the whole problem, we may agree that it should be based on real social forces in American Negro life and not on political daydreams. Foremost among such social forces are the two main population trends in American Negro history.

The first has been the vast movement in this century out of the South. For almost the entire nineteenth century, 90 per cent or more of the Negro population was concentrated in the South. The shift began to take place at about the turn of the century and took on a mass character during World War I. The percentage of Negro population in the South fell from 89.7 in 1900 to 54.4 in 1964. At the same time it rose in the North from 4.3 to 18.1, in the North-central states from 5.7 to 19.4, and in the West from 0.3 to 8.1. In effect, even if the entire South were converted into a single black nation, which no one has even thought of proposing, about half the black population would be left out of it. And if we consider the proposed Republic of New Africa, it would contain less than half the black population of the South— and less than a quarter of the black population of the country.

The second great trend has been the shift of Negro population from rural to urban areas. In the seventeenth century Negroes were brought to the United States to serve in cities as laborers and house servants. In the eighteenth century, and especially after the American Revolution, the need for slave labor in the cotton industry brought about a huge influx of Negroes into the rural South. Meanwhile, the need for unskilled labor in the North was largely filled by European immigrants. By 1890, 80 per cent of all Negroes and 85 per cent of all southern Negroes lived in rural areas. When the Negroes began to leave the South in large numbers, they headed northward to the cities. By 1960 the percentage of Negro urban population was 72.2 in the United States as a whole, 58.4 in the South, and 95.2 in the North and West.[14] By 1960, 65 per cent of all Negroes were concentrated in the sprawling metropolitan areas, 80 per cent of them in the central cities.[15] Indeed, in 1970, Negroes were more urbanized than whites.

Forecasts and projections that as many as fifty of the largest American cities would have black majorities by 1970 or that the fourteen largest American cities would have black majorities of 60 to 80 per cent by 1975 were largely based on the assumption that these population trends would continue unabated. But that assumption has proved to be unfounded. In July 1969 the Bureau of the Census reported: "The number of Negroes living in the central cities of metropolitan areas had grown steadily and sharply until very recently. An increase of 5.5 million occurred between 1950 and 1966.

However, between 1966 and 1968 the increase stopped, and there is some evidence to indicate an actual decline—constituting a sharp change in recent trends." On January 5, 1970, the Bureau of the Census confirmed that there had actually been such a decline. What seems to have happened is that, with the deterioration of the "poverty areas" in the central cities, blacks as well as whites have been fleeing from them, if they can afford to do so, though the percentage for white families was twice as large as that for blacks and other minorities. Nevertheless, this movement of some black families out of the central cities constituted a reversal of the previous trend and raised the question whether decreasing black as well as white populations will not be the fate of the urban slums.[16]

These population movements have produced baffling problems not only for the cities but for black nationalism. If the internal black migration has been from South to North and from the countryside to the cities, where is the "black nation" in the United States? Where will it be tomorrow? If it is supposed to be in the five Southern states chosen by the Republic of New Africa, it would leave out over three-quarters of the existing black population. It would go against the long-term trend of the movement of Negro population. If it is supposed to be in the cities, it would reproduce the disastrous segmentation of Pakistan on an almost ludicrous scale. The black ghettos have no viable economic existence apart from their predominantly white hinterlands; they are separated from one another, often by hundreds of miles; most of them are relatively recent, dating from World War II; and equally great changes may take place in or out of them in the next two decades, depending on economic opportunities and government policy. In any case, it is one thing for the overwhelming white majority in the country to give up residential areas to black newcomers; it would be quite another thing for the white majority to contemplate giving up state sovereignty over the same areas.

Stokely Carmichael was, as we have seen, one notable exception to the nationalist trend away from Africa in the late 1960s. Yet even he was not altogether sure. In 1969 he defended his choice of an African "land base" in these terms: "The best place, it seems to me, and the quickest place that we can obtain land is Africa. I am not denying that we might seek land in the United States. That is a possibility, but I do not see it clearly in my mind at this time. We need land and we need land immediately, and we must go to the quickest place for it." [17] But this view seemed to confuse a "land base" for a black nation and a "land base" for an international black revolutionary struggle. Ghana and quite a few nations in black Africa were quite as black without Dr. Nkrumah's leadership as they had been when he was in power. A nation may be black irrespective of its ideology, or at least a distinction should be made between black as a color and black as an ideology. Inasmuch as Carmichael conceives of African unification as meaning a single state in which "everybody speaks the same language, one government, one army," [18] his goal could be achieved only by struggling against the existing black nation-states in Africa. Moreover, it is far from clear why his conception of the unification of Africa should determine the issue whether or where the black people in America should constitute a nation. Carmichael's position implied a black civil war in Africa at least as much as a war between blacks and whites in the United States.

As matters stand, it is much easier to be a black nationalist than to know what black nationalism is. This dilemma has been created by the peculiar circumstances of American history and the peculiar conditions of American life. It may be possible for blacks and whites to move farther away from each other—but they can never move far enough to disentangle themselves from each other's fate.

Black Studies

10

The burning question is whether American black nationalism is or is not the expression of a suppressed nation. If the nationalists are right, American Negroes have always constituted a nation—without a proper nationalism. And if they are wrong, do we now have a black nationalism —without a proper nation?

Other nationalisms have rested on a persuasively simple basis. It has been the demand for sovereignty or self-rule in a particular territory. The Algerians could cry "Algeria for the Algerians"; the Indonesians demanded "Indonesia for the Indonesians." This "territorial imperative" has given every nationalism its *raison d'être* and its popular base. Algerians, as Malcolm X discovered, could be white, but they were nonetheless Algerians. The definition of an Algerian was not in his color or his class but in his relationship to his land.

Black quasi-nationalism in America, however, has been forced to look for a surrogate sovereignty, a substitute for a nation. This need is the unfulfilled and unfulfillable wish behind the demands for separate, autonomous Black or Afro-American Studies in our colleges and universities. Though Black Studies are only in a preliminary or experimental stage, we can already see what the main tendencies are and where they are heading.

The first school to introduce a Black Studies program was San Francisco State College. In the spring of 1966 it offered for the first time a class in Black Nationalism. In the academic year 1967–68 it introduced a Black Studies Curriculum consisting of eleven courses for thirty-three units of college credit.[1] Nevertheless, the situation became so inflamed that four members of the Black Students' Union invaded the college newspaper and physically assaulted the editor. Early in 1968 the President decided to appoint a Black Studies Co-ordinator, who had been chosen by the Black Students' Union. He was Dr. Nathan Hare, a black sociologist who had been too troublesome for Howard University. The atmosphere of crisis was so intense that the President saw fit to appoint him without consulting with, or even informing, the Vice-President for Academic Affairs, the Council of Academic Deans, or the faculty. He acted with such haste ostensibly to head off an "explosion," which, in the end, he merely succeeded in making worse.[2]

By the end of 1968 the Black Students' Union demanded an all-black department with the authority to grant a bachelor's degree in Black Studies and "the sole power to hire faculty and control and determine the destiny of its department." [3] It was the prototype of similar demands in one school after another. The college was shut down by a BSU student strike, which was reinforced for a time by a faculty strike called by the American Federation of Teachers. When the latter was settled, Dr. Hare wrote an article in *The Black*

Panther in which he denounced his erstwhile allies in these terms: "We can only conclude that the AFT turncoats are thieves, opportunists, lackeys, enemies of the people, and spineless. They are traitors; and students are justified should they treat them like one." [4] In a speech at Stanford University, he declared: "I was asked if I am an American first or a Negro first. I said I'm a black man first and not an American at all." If he were drafted in wartime, he said, "I couldn't fight for them [Americans], and if I did I would shoot as much as possible at the whites around me." [5] For Dr. Hare, "Black today is revolutionary and nationalistic. A Black Studies program which is not revolutionary and nationalistic is, accordingly, quite profoundly irrelevant." He once suggested that the instructor of a "Black mathematics" course might ask: "If you loot one store and burn two, how many do you have left?" [6] Dr. Hare was subsequently dismissed by the new President, Dr. S. I. Hayakawa. Another San Francisco State instructor, Jerry Varnado, in a course on "Sociology of Black Oppression," wrote out a formula for napalm so his students could "pour it on a piece of meat or on the police or somebody and see exactly how it works." [7]

At Antioch College, in Yellow Springs, Ohio, an Afro-American Studies Institute was set up from which white teachers and students were entirely excluded. In 1969 the teachers (or "consultants," as they were called) were all black Ph.D. candidates at the University of Chicago, who visited Antioch once a month for three days of classes, lecturing ten hours a day. A student spokesman for this program explained the policy of exclusionism: "For a white student to be in any of these sessions would only blunt the knife, and inhibit fundamental emotions from being expressed." He openly rejected "the idea of freedom of inquiry" as noble but unrealistic.[8] A distinguished black psychologist, Professor Kenneth B. Clark, resigned from the Antioch College Board of Trustees in protest against what he called a "charade of power." He admonished the black students that "a university could not surrender to student control a Black Studies Institute with exclusionary characteristics and without even minimal academic standards if it truly valued the humanity of blacks. If the university does not insist that Negroes be as rigorously trained as whites to compete in the arena of real power, or that studies of racism be as thoroughly and systematically pursued as studies of nuclear physics, one must question whether it is really serious." [9] *

San Francisco State College and Antioch College might be dismissed as academic aberrations. But the events at Cornell University in the spring of 1969 showed that even a major university was capable of disastrously mishandling the problem. Other schools, such as Wesleyan University in Middletown, Connecticut, went through a somewhat similar crisis, but more may perhaps be learned from the Cornell experience than from any other because the political or ideological factor came out most sharply and clearly there.

In 1963 less than twenty of Cornell's eleven thousand students were black. As the result of a policy initiated by the new president, James A. Perkins, to admit black students on the basis of more flexible criteria, about 250 black students were enrolled out of fourteen thousand in 1968–69. A minority of the black students, estimated at between fifty and one hundred, belonged to the Afro-American Society, which had been formed in 1966 and increasingly reflected the anti-integrationist, black-nationalist tendency then gaining the ascendancy. In the fall of 1968 Cornell instituted an Afro-American Studies Program, supervised by a committee composed of nine white faculty members and administrators and eight black students. The chairman of the Board of Trustees donated one million dollars to finance the new pro-

* In January 1970, however, the Afro-American Unity House, an all-black dormitory, was closed down, it was reported, by mutual agreement of the college community, black students, and the Board of Trustees (*The New York Times*, February 1, 1970).

gram. By this time, however, black-nationalist student groups throughout the country were making a coordinated drive in favor of a completely separatist Black Studies program, as at San Francisco State College, and a militant faction based on this program had won control of the AAS at Cornell.

On December 7, 1968, about fifty black militants stormed into a meeting of the program-planning committee of the Afro-American Studies Program. They proclaimed that the program and committee were through, and they appointed an all-black group to take over as the operating committee of a new "Afro-American Institute." [10] On December 12 the Afro-American Society presented President Perkins with even more far-reaching demands for a "College of Afro-American Studies." In a lengthy statement to the President and a proposed "Constitution of the College," they made clear what they understood by Black Studies at that time.

The statement took the position that the program was, in effect, a struggle for power and that power was the test of academic validity: "The validity of a program is determined by those who have the power to define and to set its limits and goals." Therefore only blacks were entitled to define and carry out the program. The only contribution whites could make was in "an advisory, non-decision making or financial capacity." As for the latter, "we expect financial aid through grants by the university, by private foundations and by endowments." In every other way, the proposed program was to have an "independent status," to select its own black professors and students, to offer its own courses, and eventually to grant its own degrees. The objective went far beyond Black Studies as such to a Black College of Black Studies: "Our aim is the creation of a Black College of Black students and scholars within a white university which will deal with the problems of Black America." This issue, the statement warned, was "no longer negotiable." In fact, the black students had already set up a fifteen-man executive committee to select a director and draw up a constitution for the new Black College.[11] The proposed constitution set forth the college's objective in unmistakably nationalist terms: "This College has been organized to prepare Black students to deal with the problems of the Black Nation and to offer services and benefits for the improvement of the Black Nation." [12] *

From this time on, Cornell struggled with the problem of Black Studies under duress. In December 1968 the administration and faculty refused to go along with the demand for an independent black college. But President Perkins began to deal with the Afro-American Society as if it were the recognized bargaining agency of all the black students and, indeed, represented the black viewpoint in general. In a memorandum addressed to the AAS, he explained that the fundamental problem was the issue of the proposed program's "complete autonomy." Ironically, he committed himself to a number of educational principles, such as faculty responsibility for academic standards, that would have made such a self-contained enclave impossible. Nevertheless, he went on to accept the sidetracking of the existing Afro-American Studies Program as an accomplished fact. He took

* There is in existence a memorandum which was quoted by John Hatch, "Black Studies: The Real Issue," in *The Nation*, June 16, 1969, p. 757. This memorandum, drawn up by black students at Cornell, but not otherwise identified, worked out a Black Studies program "to enable Black people to use the knowledge gained in the classroom and the community to formulate new ideologies and philosophies which will contribute to the development of the Black nation." As part of such a program, the memorandum listed Course 300c in Physical Education: "Theory and practice in the use of small arms and hand to hand combat. Discussions in the proper use of force" (Tentative Course Outline, p. 3). I am indebted to Mr. Hatch for a copy of this memorandum. An "Outline of the Curricula for the Department of Afro-American Studies," prepared by the Executive Planning Committee of the Black Students' Alliance at the State University of New York at Albany, January 1969, listed as requirements for all graduate students: "Mastery of ONE of the following disciplines: A) Basic reading knowledge of either Swahili, Yoruba, Arabic, Spanish, Portuguese, or Chinese. B) Sufficient mastery of either Akido, Karate, Gung Fu, Judo, Riflery, or Stick Fighting" (p. 2).

the trouble to assure the AAS that the new program "should have a Black Director who would be acceptable to Afro-American students." Yet he also felt it necessary to state that he personally did not favor "a completely independent organization" and still hoped for a program "in which Whites and Blacks can work together in peace and understanding." [13]

Thereupon, in effect, the Cornell administration began to negotiate directly with the AAS for a new Black Studies program. When some faculty members protested against its autonomous features, they were not asked for their views again.[14] On April 10, 1969, the new plan was publicly unveiled. It provided for an inter-college Center for Afro-American Studies, headed by a director directly responsible to the President. The AAS was effectively permitted to choose the director, who was assured of at least associate professor rank. In May, after protracted bargaining, the post went to James E. Turner, a twenty-eight-year-old graduate student in sociology at Northwestern University, where he had been a prominent black nationalist student leader. When Mr. Turner was appointed, no one as yet knew just what the Center was supposed to do or what Mr. Turner's ideas were. Five months after his appointment, a special trustee committee saw fit to recommend that the administration should request Mr. Turner to make a detailed statement of his plans, including curriculum, course study content, budget, etc.[15]

Meanwhile, the black students' tactics were becoming more and more forceful. In December 1968 some of them went on a spree with toy guns, as the student paper called it, clogged the return bins of several libraries with hundreds of books taken off the shelves, and appropriated furniture from a women's dormitory for the AAS headquarters. In the early morning hours of April 19, 1969, about twenty-four hours after a cross was discovered burning on the porch of a black women's dormitory, they routed employees and parents out of bed in Willard Straight Hall. When a rumor spread that evening that armed whites were going to assault them, they brought guns into the building. Thirty-six hours later, the Vice-President for Public Affairs, the Vice-Provost, and two top AAS leaders, surrounded by the gun-bearing black students, onlookers, and the press, solemnly signed a formal agreement making the necessary concessions to the AAS in return for evacuation of the building. The black students, triumphantly carrying their guns, marched in military formation to the AAS headquarters. When the full faculty failed to ratify the agreement on April 21, one black leader, Tom Jones, speaking on the Cornell-owned radio station, warned that President Perkins, four top administrators, and three professors "will be dealt with" and gave the university "three hours to live." At a meeting on the evening of April 22, Jones also declared publicly: "Now the pigs are going to die too . . . people like J. P. [President Perkins] . . . are going to be dealt with. . . . We are moving tonight. Cornell has until 9 to live." [16] Some faculty members received anonymous telephone calls and at least one moved his family for the night.[17] In the face of these threats, the faculty reversed itself the following day. The faculty's about-face within forty-eight hours proved to be the turning point of the immediate crisis. Several outstanding faculty members resigned in protest against the administration's handling of the problem, and President Perkins himself made known his resignation on May 31.

A month later, on June 29, 1969, Tom Jones made a speech to summer-school students at Willard Straight Hall in which he explained what had happened at Cornell for the past year. "I'm speaking to you tonight," he began, "because I expect that possibly if you understand what's happening, you might put yourselves in the way of stopping it so we can go on about our development as individuals and *as a Black nation*." * Then he told what had inspired him and his followers: "The purpose of our Black Studies program was number one, to give us that psychological freedom of self-definition, to define what we are now, what we have

* Italics in this paragraph are mine.—T.D.

been as a people, and what we will be as a people and *as a nation in the future*. The second purpose of the Black Studies program was to teach us the political methods, the political ideology to lead to the kind of political freedom and economic self-determination that we have to have." For these purposes, he went on, they had decided on a number of "persuasive steps" to force the university "to have them recognize what had to be for our lives, not only here in Ithaca and on the campus of Cornell University, but *as a Black nation*."

As for the takeover of Willard Straight Hall, it had been planned in advance, and the cross-burning had merely provided a convenient occasion for doing what they had intended to do anyway. "Now, our action was planned to occur at a critical juncture for Cornell: namely, Parents Weekend. Parents Weekend simply because for us to take the action at that time meant that we couldn't be ignored by the university." In reply to a question, he went into greater detail about the planning:

> The whole issue with the disciplinary board had been taking place from a period in late January-early February right up until April with Parents Weekend. So, of course, you know, recognizing the possibility that the judicial boards and the faculty were going to try to suppress us and engage in this act of political repression, plans had made, plans had been made, you know. But it's not as if the Straight was taken over on the spur-of-the-moment. And it's not as if plans had been made to take over the Straight and the judicial issue was just, you know, a convenient thing.*

There was no doubt in Jones's mind that the display of guns had forced the university's hand: "What happened now that the university knew that we had guns in here, see

---

* Of six black students charged with misconduct in the events of December 1968, the Faculty Committee on Student Affairs decided on April 18, 1969, to mete out "reprimands" to three only for their part in the toy-gun affair. This "penalty" involved no more than letters to the students' parents and dean.

they got very, very rushed. Very, very rushed. And why, why? Because they knew . . . they knew that at this point the lives of white students were in jeopardy." In fact, he strongly hinted that some of the faculty members had had good cause to fear that violence might be done to them: "So the first step we took in changing reality was to make clear to them, to specific people that had been instrumental in getting the faculty to reject the agreement, we made it clear to them . . . we said it over the radio, we said, you're racist and you're going to be dealt with. Said you put me against the wall, you backed me into a corner, you're trying to destroy me, well if you believe in your principle sufficiently, if you believe in it to that point, then be ready to die for it." And all this had been acted out for the benefit of a much larger audience, for, as Jones put it, "that moment was a moment in history with Black people marching out of the Student Union at Cornell University in military formation, that was a moment that's going down in history . . . that was a moment that galvanized Black people across this nation." [18]

Was it such a great black victory? Professor Clark did not think so. He had no illusions about the balance of forces at Cornell, if the whites had chosen to use their power:

> The armed black students at Cornell had no real power—not they, but the white majority were in control. The fact that the white administration and faculty chose not to act violently in response, but rather to acquiesce—or appear to acquiesce—to demands, did not obscure the evidence of real power. The guns at the ready were a charade; they were permitted only because the majority understood they could be put down whenever it wished to do so. To the extent that whites encourage in blacks acceptance of this pretense of power, they are participating in but one more manifestation of an old racism.[19]

Clearly, then, the gun incident at Cornell—which *The Black Panther* headlined as: "Power At Cornell Out Of The

Barrel Of A Gun" [20]—could be interpreted in more than one way. The danger in such symbolic dramatizations is that they may lead the more violent black nationalists into misreading the actual relationship of forces in the country. If Professor Clark is right, white officials who encourage such self-deception, even if for the best reasons, may be doing their black students no favor. In any case, the Cornell confrontation could not have developed so disastrously without a self-conscious nationalist element deeply imbedded in it— and without the inability of Cornell officials to recognize or deal with it.

Cornell has had to live with its new Black Studies program, now headed by Mr. Turner. In August 1969 he published an article in which he gave his views on "Black Students and Their Changing Perspective." The goal of the black struggle, he wrote, was "self-determination." This struggle sought to provide blacks "with a collective economic base and political control over land." The "motif" of the struggle was "ideas of racial solidarity, nation-building and self-determination." The black student movement "has moved the road to liberation for black people onto a new plateau of black nationalism." The demand for Black Studies now and a Black University to come was "opposed to the traditionally Negro colleges which reflect the curriculum of white institutions." [21]

All these ideas or slogans have become the common currency of black nationalist thought, but one merits special attention. It is the distinction between "Black" and "Negro," here applied to higher education. As we have noted, Black is not merely a color; it is an ideology. There are one hundred twenty-eight predominantly Negro colleges, with, in 1969, about one hundred thirty thousand students, approximately half the total number of black undergraduates. Nevertheless, from this point of view these institutions might just as well be white because they cannot pass the political test of "blackness." Ironically, a relatively few ideologically self-certified blacks in predominantly white schools have given themselves the power to decide who is and who is not truly "black." They may even decide that some whites with the right ideology are blacker than blacks with the wrong ideology. Those in possession of the ideology can decide for the people or even without the people by making those who disagree with them un-people, or, as in this case, un-blacks. Out of such ideologies have come modern totalitarian movements and party dictatorships.

The full ideology of academic black nationalism is being worked out at the Institute of the Black World at Atlanta, Georgia. It is headed by Dr. Vincent Harding, a history professor at Spelman College in Atlanta, as part of the Martin Luther King, Jr., Memorial Center. Dr. Harding thinks of his institute as "a kind of international center for black studies"; another view is that he wishes to make it "the Vatican of black studies with himself as the Pope." [22] Indeed, Dr. Harding's ambition goes far beyond Black Studies. He has set forth the goal as nothing less than "that all the study of America and the world be saturated with the significance of the black presence"; that it bring about "a new definition of America and its institutions, a total re-evaluation from a Black perspective"; and "the total reorganization of university knowledge and curriculum from a Black perspective." This implies far more than black nationalist control of Black Studies; it entails the substitution of a total black perspective for a total white perspective. Dr. Harding has also hinted that Black Studies should take in "black science" as well as black social studies and humanities.[23]

Dr. Harding, however, has not gone as far as Stokely Carmichael. In 1969 the latter gave this prescription for a black university: "In the United States, a black university, a truly black university, is going to be totally anti-American, not just possibly anti-American, but anti-American to the point where it urges people to destroy, dismantle, disrupt, tear down, level completely in America. So you cannot have that, but that is precisely the job of the black educator, to train his people how to dismantle America, how to destroy it." [24]

In the summer of 1969 the Institute of the Black World held a six-week Workshop on Black Studies for thirty-one selected all-black teachers and students, one of them Cornell's Mr. Turner. In October of that year Mr. Turner finally submitted a plan for his Center for Afro-American Studies, which he had renamed the Africana Studies and Research Center. The basis of his plan, he stated, was derived largely from documents developed at the institute and distributed at the workshop. [25]

Mr. Turner also hoped to create "an international center for Black Studies" at Cornell. In his view, Black Studies included technology and science as well as black history and culture. The program ultimately aimed to prepare "a new cadre of intellectuals" and "a new kind of professional school." He envisaged a "home center" at Cornell and an "Urban Resident Center" in a black community elsewhere. Each center would have a separate faculty, with "free interchange" among them. Students would be expected to spend the first two years on academic work at the Cornell Center, a third year at the urban center, and a fourth probably writing a thesis on the previous year's project. Crucial to the entire plan was the choice and commitment of these students:

> While seriously considering such factors as academic training and standing, we must place the greatest reliance on the candidate's relevance to the Black community and his commitment to work towards the solution of its problems. We have neither the time nor resources to operate a race-relations project wherein well-meaning but inexperienced and dysfunctional White students would occupy positions that might better be filled by Blacks. Of course, relevant and equally well-qualified (background, experience, commitment) Whites are welcome, but such qualified candidates will undoubtedly be rare.

They were so rare that they numbered less than 2 per cent of the first class of about 160 in the fall semester of 1969.

Mr. Turner conceded that Cornell might also admit black students interested in the university's traditional program. He was solely concerned with the "second stream of Black students," so little interested in the traditional education that, he said, they would probably not consider going to college at all if his program did not exist. By 1972, he expected, the Center would grant its own degrees for a sequence of courses based on its own curriculum. To make the Center completely self-contained, he excluded joint appointments with Cornell's academic departments and insisted on a "centralized faculty" appointed directly to and by the Center itself. Cornell has committed itself for three years to a minimum of $215,000 annually for the Center and an additional $25,000 for research and development of the urban component.

If this plan should succeed at Cornell and elsewhere, it may well produce a "new cadre of intellectuals," or at least a new cadre of black nationalist organizers and propagandists. If Dr. Harding and Mr. Turner were to head a new black nationalist party, its Black Studies program might not be very different from the one introduced at Cornell, with the latter having the added advantage of being able to grant a degree from a major university. In fact, the program outlined for the Africana Studies and Research Center would prepare its students for little else than to devote themselves professionally to "racial solidarity, nation-building, and self-determination," as Mr. Turner put it in his August 1969 article. The new black nationalist elite has not been able to adapt itself to organizations like the Black Panthers, many of whose members literally come from the *Lumpenproletariat*. The other nationalist organizations already have entrenched leaderships, which betray no desire to share power. These Black Schools of Black Studies may not be able to create a new black nation, but it is hard to see how they can fail to produce new black nationalists.

A different procedure was followed at Yale University. In 1964, fourteen of Yale's 1050 freshmen were black. That fall the fourteen organized themselves informally into the Black Student Alliance at Yale, primarily for social reasons. As more black students were admitted, a Yale Discussion Group on Negro Affairs was formed during the 1965–66 school year. The BSAY sponsored its first "issue-oriented" conference in the spring of 1966. It began to focus its attention on the Yale curriculum in the fall of 1967. By February of the following year, meetings were being held with President Kingman Brewster, Jr., other top administrators, and faculty members. As a result, President Brewster appointed a committee, later known as the African-American Study Group, made up of four faculty and four BSAY members. This committee worked out proposals for an undergraduate, interdisciplinary program in Afro-American studies. This program, it was agreed, should not "operate as a black hegemony," or attempt to set up a separate department. The committee decided to base it on the area-studies model and to make it "rigorous" in character. Administration of the program was entrusted to a faculty committee representing the various departments and special studies programs. Of the seven guidelines set down for the committee, the first read: "Direction of the program to conform to the academic standards of Yale College." Teaching personnel were required to have appointments in one of the formal disciplines on which the course of study was based. Qualified white as well as black students and faculty were provided for. The Yale College faculty unanimously approved a degree-granting Afro-American studies program, the first at a major American university, on December 12, 1968.[26]

When the program was initiated in September 1969, by which time there were over a hundred black undergraduates at Yale, the chairman of its faculty committee, Professor Sidney W. Mintz, set forth its four principal features as follows:

1. The Afro-American heritage and contemporary Afro-American societies and cultures are to be studied in their total hemispheric diversity and richness, while the role of Africa in the past and present of Afro-American culture and consciousness will be thoroughly explored;

2. strong course emphasis in some specific discipline (such as Anthropology, Economics, English Literature, History, Political Science or Sociology) is required, in order to provide each student with a substantive disciplinary grounding, and to equip him best for future graduate and professional training;

3. active research in the field and/or in documentary and secondary sources is an integral part of the advanced training required by the majors and will normally be conducted during the summer between the junior and senior years;

4. the writing of a senior research essay under the supervision of a faculty adviser is an essential of degree completion; the essay will be based upon studies realized during the junior year and the following summer, and will be written during the senior year.[27]

These features are as significant for what they exclude as much as for what they include. There is nothing in them that suggests a black-nationalist party line. Thus fundamental differences can already be detected in the various Black Studies programs. One type may rightly be called Black Studies and the other type should be called Black Nationalist Studies—which is not the same as the study of black nationalism. There is, to be sure, room for nationalist-minded students and even teachers in a Black Studies program, in much the same way that representatives of different schools of thought may be represented in other fields of study. The nationalist orientation gives itself away by one-sidedness, discrimination, and exclusionism. It discriminates against anti-separatist black students and teachers as well as against qualified white students and teachers. The ideal program in this as in other fields should close no options and open all possible horizons. Otherwise, Black Studies may easily degenerate into the training of cadres for an incipient black nationalist party.

Black Nationalist Studies constitute one more expression of the fantasy-nationalism we have been surveying. They demand all the trappings of "self-determination," except the ability to pay for themselves. Yet the more deeply they penetrate into white academic territory, the more profoundly they withdraw into themselves. They want sovereignty, but a subsidized sovereignty. They seek to develop the rudiments of a new black nation, but merely succeed in producing a new form of black ghetto. They cannot break the umbilical cord with the white world, and they cannot live harmoniously within that world.

By no means do I wish to challenge the validity and necessity of Black Studies. The more we know about "black history," "black literature," or "black sociology," the better it will be for all of us. By Black Studies, I mean nothing more than the history of black people or the sociology of black communities, not a "black history" or a "black sociology" so different in kind that only blacks can understand or use them. The real question is whether these should be studied and taught the way other subjects are studied and taught, as a collective educational enterprise, or whether they should be studied and taught with a built-in nationalist mystique outside the bounds of rational discourse and authentic scholarship. This nationalist bias invariably leads to the insistence that Black Studies must be organized into a self-governing, all-black department from which white students may be excluded. Whether a department or an interdepartmental program is better for these studies is, to my mind, not the main point, though departments lend themselves to autonomy far more than interdepartmental programs. The crucial question is whether the Black Studies set-up should imply that blacks and whites in the United States belong to two different nations, one long established, the other striving to be born, and should treat each other as such in universities, trade unions, and ultimately everywhere else. The set-up is therefore tremendously important to black nationalists, who demand departments or even schools that could act as if they were *ersatz* foreign institutions with extraterritorial rights.

The nationalist case for Black Studies in white schools is marked by a curious contradiction. According to the nationalist party line, all whites are hopelessly racist, white schools merely mirror a racist society, "white culture" is not "relevant" to the "black experience," and separatism is the only way out. If so, it may be asked, what are Black Studies doing in white schools? The answer is that black nationalists do not really want them to be part of those schools; they want to re-create black schools in, but not of, white schools.

We are only in the first phase of this peculiar symbiosis. Ultimately, white schools may not be able to evade responsibility for the kind of black nationalism they may be, wittingly or unwittingly, sponsoring. If, as Turner says, black "nation-building" has become the motif of the struggle, the result can only be nation-disintegrating—of the present American nation. In the end, Black Studies may greatly help to provide both blacks and whites with more knowledge of and greater clarity about their problems, but only if these studies do not foreclose the search for answers by dedicating themselves in advance to some extreme form of black nationalism.

It is important to recognize that the case for Black Studies is not the same as the case for Black Schools of Black Studies. The case for Black Studies rests on the intrinsic validity and significance of the subject matter; the case for Black Schools of Black Studies is less concerned with white schools than with white money. In the end, a marriage of convenience will benefit neither the white school nor Black Studies. A set-up which exacerbates existing differences and antagonisms could in the long run set back Black Studies for a generation.

In a symposium held at Yale University in 1967 but published two years later, one black sociologist argued: "If there are black people in this society that live in segregated institutions, that's exactly what you have to create on the university campus." [28] Apart from all other considerations, why go to all that trouble when there are already so many segregated black institutions in the United States? What is the point of getting physically closer together in order to get psychologically further apart? I have no doubt that Black Studies in hitherto white schools are fully justified and long overdue—but only if they lessen the gap between whites and blacks, help break down the walls of prejudice and ignorance, give each the benefit of the other. In the interest of the entire society, white students need Black Studies as much as or even more than black students. In an educational sense, "Black" should refer to what is being studied, not who is studying and who is teaching.[29]

Thus far we have been thinking in terms of blacks and whites. But we must also think of Black Studies in terms of blacks and blacks. The idea of Black Studies by and for blacks only tends to assume that there is something in the nature of a monolithic black consciousness, which can or will express itself in these studies. This is by no means the case. Blacks differ among themselves as much as they may differ with whites; the extreme nationalist tendency is only one of many, and the nationalists are far from united on what they stand for. The problem then becomes: which blacks are going to decide what Black Studies should be? The politicalization of Black Studies almost fatally makes them a battleground for rival black movements and ideologies. "Battleground" here is no mere metaphor. The struggle for control of the Afro-American Studies Center at the University of California at Los Angeles went so far that two Black Panther leaders who were also students at UCLA were shot to death on January 17, 1969, in the university's Campbell Hall. They were Alprentice "Bunchy" Carter, Deputy Minister of Defense, and John Jerome Huggins, Deputy Minister of Information, both of southern California.[30] In the next four months two more Panthers were killed in San Diego.[31] These murders were ascribed to a rival nationalist outfit headed by "Maulana" Ron Karenga (born Ronald Everett), who founded the organization US (as opposed to "them") in 1965. (Karenga means "keeper of the tradition" and "Maulana" is an honorific title in Arabic.) The Panthers were so incensed at the deaths of Carter and Huggins in Los Angeles that they provided the police with the photographs of the four alleged US assailants and the names of three others.[32] Five US members were indicted, of whom three were sentenced to life imprisonment. To the Panthers, Karenga represents the most dangerous of the pseudo-African "cultural nationalists," and their enmity could make a shambles of the Afro-American Studies Center even if the directorship were not so lucrative and Panther blood had not been shed.

Black Studies as such offer no insuperable problems for American schools. Given the will, the way can be found. But Black Studies of, by, and for black nationalism are a different kind of problem. Writing about the Vietnam war, Eldridge Cleaver once referred to black Americans as "a Black Trojan Horse within white America." [33] This is the language of war, not of peaceful coexistence. If Black Studies attempt to play that role in white schools, one or the other must surrender. In the present circumstances, it is not at all certain that "nation-building" Black Studies are strong enough to be victorious.

Limits

11

From one point of view, it would be much easier and simpler if there were such a thing as a "black colony" or a "black nation" in the United States. At least it would clearly define the problem and point to its solution. Perhaps the most difficult and baffling aspect of the American Negro problem is that it has no such clarity and no such definition. The black "land question" is made up of enclaves and ghettos, which can only rhetorically be called a nation or nations. As soon as the term "colonialism" is applied to the American Negro experience, it is necessary to add the qualifier, "a special variety," the variety being so special that it admittedly lacks a colonial territory or economy.[1] When "nation" and "colony" are used so loosely to cover so much ground, they raise more questions than they answer, lose all the sharpness and force of their traditional meaning, or else say one thing and mean another.

A starting point may be the frank recognition that it is easier to say what the American Negro is not than what he is. If he does not constitute a nation of the Third World type, is he merely another one of America's well-known ethnic groups, such as the Irish, the Italian, or the Jewish? The ethnic label also strikes me as unsatisfactory and misleading. While the national concept seems to go too far, the ethnic concept does not seem to go far enough. No ethnic group in American history has suffered degradation and discrimination so rigid and so lasting as those established by the color line. While the ethnic ghettos have decreased or disappeared, Negro ghettos have enormously increased and enlarged. Indeed, it is the specific and intransigent character of the Negro problem that has given rise to the black nationalism we have been considering. America's ethnic groups gladly left another nationalism behind them; only the Negro has had to invent a spurious nationalism to cope with his extraordinary condition.

If black America is not a nation, what is it? No term has yet seemed exactly suitable. "Race" has been used for a long time, for want of something better, despite its dubious biological connotations. "Class" is not much better because the Negro problem cuts across class lines. In the late 1930s a "caste-class" school of thought arose. This caste system was based on color, but within each of the castes, white and black, social classes prevailed.[2] But this analysis applied only to the South; "ethnic" generally replaced "caste" for the North. Gunnar Myrdal and his associates did not even bother to consider whether the American Negroes constituted a nation, and they found fault with "minority group" (which they treated as the equivalent of "ethnic group"), "race," and "class." In the end they preferred the term "caste" as coming closest to the American reality.[3] But critics of the caste interpretation protested that it was too static or underplayed the "class" factor.[4] In one of his most challenging insights, however, Myrdal struck at the primitive

source of the problem: "Should America wake up one morning with all knowledge about the African ancestry of part
of its population and all the outward physical characteristics
of the Negro people eradicated, but no change in their
mental or moral characteristics, nothing we know about this
group and other population groups in America would lead
us to believe that the American Negro would not rapidly
come to fit in as a well-adjusted ordinary American." In this
sense, as he said, it is "a white man's problem." [5]

Without pretending to pass judgment on this delicate and
difficult issue, what strikes me most of all is the many-sided
specificity of the American Negro problem. It breaks out of
one conceptual compartment after another and yet defies
a synthesis of all of them. The Negro group is a "minority"
—but it is unlike all other minority groups. It is a "class"
for the vast majority of its members—but it extends beyond
the class line. It has some likeness to a "caste"—but it does
not have the religious sanction on which the classical system of Hinduism in India rests. The only thing to do with
such a phenomenon is to see it for itself and not to make
it something else.* American history (especially the appall-

* No one has better expressed the individuality and complexity of the
American Negroes' position than the novelist and essayist James
Baldwin, who wrote: "But in order to change a situation one has first
to see it for what it is: in the present case, to accept the fact, whatever one does with it thereafter, that the Negro has been formed by
this nation, for better or for worse, and does not belong to any other
—not to Africa, and certainly not to Islam. The paradox—and a fear-
ful paradox it is—is that the American Negro can have no future
anywhere, on any continent, as long as he is unwilling to accept his
past. To accept one's past—one's history—is not the same thing as
drowning in it; it is learning how to use it. An invented past can never
be used; it cracks and crumbles under the pressures of life like clay
in a season of drought. How can the American Negro's past be used?
The unprecedented price demanded—and at this embattled hour of
the world's history—is the transcendence of the realities of color, of
nations, and of altars." In another passage, Baldwin wrote: "The
American Negro is a unique creation; he has no counterpart anywhere, and no predecessors" (*The Fire Next Time,* first published New
York: Dial Press, 1963, reprinted Penguin Books, 1964, pp. 71–73).

ingly incompatible heritage of slavery and democracy), the distribution of population, the ever more interdependent and interlocking economy, are among the circumstances that have molded the American Negro problem in ways that are both like and unlike any other. The colonial or national metaphor may be mistaken, but it evokes enough of the reality to be persuasive to those who are desperately looking for a neat and simple "revolutionary" answer. If fantasy is a substitute for reality, then the fantasy of black nationalism should help us to understand better the reality for which it is a substitute.

Those who do not take account of the nationalist fantasy are bound to get hurt, as even the presumably more knowledgeable white New Left sponsors of the New Politics Conference in Chicago discovered in 1967. This conference, set up to work out a New Left strategy for the 1968 presidential election, was attended by about 2500 delegates, of whom about one-tenth were black. The latter formed a Black Caucus, which proceeded to deliver ultimata to the entire conference in which they hardly deigned to take part. First they made two peremptory demands with a time limit for acceptance—that the Black Caucus should be given representation equal to all the whites on the steering and other committees, and that the convention should adopt a 13-point program reflecting "black revolutionary consciousness." After much tormented oratory, the convention capitulated to both demands by a vote of nearly three to one. This demonstration of "liberal sincerity" was thereupon further tested by a third demand, going still further, that the Black Caucus be given conference votes equal to that of the entire white majority. After even more tormented oratory, the third ultimatum was accepted by more than two to one. The conference thereupon sealed its fate and came to a sad, bitter, demoralized end. The larger New Left has not yet recovered from this fiasco.[6]

One white sponsor of the organization, who in the end rebelled against the Black Caucus's tactics, wrote that the 13 points were "incredible" and the will of the Black Caucus was "irrational." [7] These were, to be sure, "incredible" and "irrational" to him and others in his painfully awkward position. But a black nationalist could make them credible and rational. "When the representatives of two nations sit down to negotiate their common or conflicting interests, they meet as equals and the guiding principle is 'one nation, one vote,'" expounded Eldridge Cleaver. "Seen in this light, the demand of the Black Caucus at Chicago for 50 per cent of the votes is only an assertion of equal national status." [8] He did not bother to explain how the Black Caucus came to represent the black nation or the white delegates the white nation. It was enough that blacks were in a position to make take-it-or-leave-it demands on whites; this parody of national "negotiations" was worthy of a fantasy-nationalism capable neither of representing a real nation nor of conducting real negotiations.

From the outset, however, there have been two sides to this fantasy, as I have tried to show. The white colonizationists of the nineteenth century did not think that whites and blacks could live together and therefore drew the conclusion that it was necessary to induce at least the free Negroes to leave the country. That premise is still with us, even if a different conclusion has in practice been drawn from it. The physical separation of whites from blacks has taken place within rather than outside the country. The colonizationist impulse has lived on but has taken other forms.

A divisiveness so old and so deep cannot be easily dealt with or lightly brushed aside. Whatever it is, it is there, it has been there for a long time, and it has a protean capacity for survival. That whites and blacks in the United States cannot live wholly apart does not mean that they can or will —for the foreseeable future—live wholly together. As usual, the desirable and the possible are not altogether compatible, and it may be necessary for everyone's sake to steer a course between them. To chart such a course, it is often useful to delimit the outer boundaries of where it is humanly feasible to go. In extreme cases, it is useful to know where not to go, even if we cannot be sure just where to go.

One of the most depressing diagnoses of the problem was made by W. H. Ferry, a former Fellow of the Center for the Study of Democratic Institutions at Santa Barbara, California. He must be given credit for one of the few efforts to think the problem through to the bitter end without cant and without inhibitions. His first article, which attracted the most attention, was obviously not intended to be taken too literally, as its title, "Black Colonies: A Modest Proposal," hinted. In it, he maintained that the real relationship between whites and blacks in the United States was "one of colonialism: a subject people and their governors." To make this *de facto* condition of black America *de jure,* he proposed "the formal establishment of a system of black colonies in the United States," with a Department of Colonial Affairs in Washington, D.C., headed by a Secretary of Cabinet rank. To qualify as a colony, an area would need to be no more than a mile square with a population of twenty-five thousand, at least 75 per cent black. A Statute of Colonization would permit blacks to travel outside their colonies, but only on condition that they should suffer discrimination without complaint. On the other hand, a Reciprocal Indignities Understanding would subject whites in the black colonies to similar treatment. "Thus black colonists will be free to whistle at white women, deny normal services to whites and overcharge them when services are provided, expect their police to regard all whites as suspicious persons and mistreat them accordingly, and deny whites access to clubs and rest rooms." [9]

In a subsequent article he developed his ideas somewhat less coyly. He advanced three basic propositions: that the major American cities would become preponderantly black in less than a generation; that "racial integration" in the United States was impossible because whites did not want it; and that "the United States has at best a few years of grace to think through a political theory that will at once maintain democratic practice and institutions and provide for an ethnically separated minority community." Toward this end, Mr. Ferry explicitly rejected a number of possible directions. One was reliance on science and technology to provide a miraculous cure, such as a simple change of pigmentation. Another was the old colonizationist and emigrationist schemes. A third excluded systematic repression and violence. Moreover, he now clearly repudiated the notion of internal colonies that he had previously played with: "I find equally distasteful, though some political theorists may not, the idea of formalizing the separateness of the races by establishing colonies of blacks within this country. It must be recognized that urban blacktowns already fit most descriptions of colonies. But the idea is blighted from the outset by the obsolescence of colonialism as a respectable political relationship."

The stakes, Mr. Ferry warned, were very high. They were nothing less than "the preservation of the Union," as they had been over a century ago. Far from wanting another irrepressible conflict, he hoped to avoid one: "The theory we are seeking is not a plan of battle but a plan for peaceful coexistence." He called for a "creative federalism" which eschewed both the goals of integration and apartheid. What then? He seemed to envision a "separate state" or an "autonomous and self-governing community" of blacks. We have little more here than the bare notion of a new federal structure based on "autonomous" white and black "states," somehow linked and somehow separate. Unlike the first article, the second one did not try to define the area or population necessary to constitute a black "state," but the context strongly implied that it would be made up primarily of the dispersed urban centers in which blacks have a majority. The rest would have to be worked out by a new "philosophy and machinery for democratic government of a separated country." Otherwise, the prospect could not be more ominous: "The requirement is to agree on the terms of peaceful coexistence. Unless we can find them, the second Civil War is inevitable." [10]

Mr. Ferry seemed to have gone right up to the extreme limits of separatism—and tried to stop. Whether any "federalism" could be much more than an adhesive plaster on a torn and bleeding body politic strikes me as very doubtful. Yet he has not been the only one to raise the essential point that something must give—and is giving. In a lecture at Williamsburg, Virginia, on June 1, 1968, George F. Kennan asked whether it would not be necessary to permit the American Negro "first to have, as a number of his leaders are now demanding, a local political community of his own through which he can find his identity and gain the dignity of both authority and responsibility." If this "local political community" were to remain an integral part of the United States, whatever its relationship to the other parts might be, it would still fail to satisfy the yearnings of black nationalism for a black nation. But the idea pointed in the direction of enabling the "nationalist mood," as Harold Cruse called it, to find an outlet locally in those areas which are preponderantly black anyway.

The idea of black "city-states" has also been put forward by some black nationalists. The proponents of this idea, according to one informed source, divide into two schools of thought: "One segment of the City-Statesman group envisions the American politico-economic structure as legitimate and thus seeks to enter it by initially withdrawing and building the blackening cities into politically and economically powerful quasi-autonomous city-states destined to vie for influence and control of white America's capital and resources. The other segment believes that black cities can be simultaneously independently autonomous of the American politico-economic structure and also exist within it as communal (non-capitalist) city-states." Some such idea seems to be behind the Community Development Corporation sponsored by the Congress of Racial Equality (CORE) to gain black control over all funds coming into black communities. Some also believe in working through the Democratic or Republican parties as "black blocs"; others prefer a third party, either all-black or a "black/radical-white coalition party." The more extreme black nationalists have scoffed at these views on the ground that such black "city-states" could never become independent of white economic and political control. One such critic, who found good reasons to reject "integrationism," city-states, Back-to-Africa-ism, and a new Black Nation, finally decided that Revolutionary Nationalism demanded that *"America as it exists today must be completely destroyed and then rebuilt in the terms of the New Black Man"* (italics in original).[11] The *Black Manifesto,* proclaimed in April 1969 by the National Black Economic Development Conference, headed by James Forman, similarly called on black Americans to "liberate all the people in the U.S." and to "think in terms of the total control of the U.S." [12] This variety of black nationalism, which need not be taken too seriously, seeks to solve the problem of how to give the black "city-states" a self-sufficient economic infrastructure by laying claim to the entire United States.

Is not the question, then: What are the limits within which black people can feel that they are asserting their individuality and determining their own fate?

These limits must still be found. It would be futile to set them forth in advance. A great deal, as Mr. Ferry suggests, may come about tacitly. In some ways we are living through a second Reconstruction in order to avoid a second Civil War. Whatever the best answer may be, we will get closer to it if we know what the problem is—and what it is not. If we assume, with the black nationalists, that the problem is how to give birth to a black nation within the United States, the answer can only be devastating for both sides. This problem contains a built-in answer of hopeless, irreconcilable, indeterminate civil strife. One side cannot win, and the other side has everything to lose.

How much "autonomy" and "self-governing" can a "local political community" of blacks have without breaking the integument of the Union? One answer is that it can have at least as much as other distinctive groups have had. In the American tradition, this is considerable. In order to deprive black communities in the South of representation of their choosing, it was hitherto necessary to deprive most blacks of the right to vote or to gerrymander districts to make their votes unavailing. Now that black communities have begun to elect black officials, we have entered a new testing period to find out whether the rules of the democratic game apply equally to blacks and whites. The life of Charles Evers may well be one of the most important lives in the United States. This is not merely a problem of democracy for blacks; it is a trial of existing white democracy. We still do not know how much of the trouble can be assuaged by making the existing democratic rules apply to blacks and whites alike, or how much the rules need to be stretched to enable the black community to catch up or at least to close the gap between blacks and whites. Both of these processes seem to be at work. The "rules"—or, in any case, their interpretation—have been stretched before, and can be stretched again. But if they are being stretched in order to tear them asunder, they are more likely to rebound than to break.

For example, something new has been taking place in East Palo Alto, California. Of the 27,000 residents in this community, near Stanford University, two-thirds are black. In April 1968 a campaign was launched to change the name from East Palo Alto to Nairobi, after the capital of Kenya. The proposal was voted down in the November 1968 election by 3052 to 1262. Nevertheless, the San Mateo County district attorney ruled that East Palo Alto was not a name with legal status and hence could be changed through common usage. This has been happening. There is a "Nairobi Village Shopping Center," owned by Counterpart, an organization of black and white businessmen. The center contains a Nairobi Village Cleaners, an Oja Nairobi boutique, a Nairobi Book Store, and other shops. There is also a Nairobi Day School, a Nairobi High School, and, in the planning stage, a Nairobi College.[13]

Where is such a phenomenon heading? Is it the microcosm of a new black community or the embryo of a new black nation? The first may coexist and even cooperate peacefully with the larger neighboring white community; the second will certainly bring on ultimately undefinable and irreconcilable conflicts between them. Any consideration of future trends must take into account the extreme volatility of the black "mood" in the 1960s. In 1964 the tendency was overwhelmingly "integrationist." Five years later, "integrationism" had become a bad word, and some form of "separatism" —cultural, political, or both—was all the rage, especially in black intellectual and youthful circles. Such a spasmodic shift may or may not represent the long-term will or interest of the black majority. An extremist, militant minority succeeded in temporarily gaining the public ascendancy in the black community. Much of this public ascendancy was made possible, ironically, by white media of communications. As in intelligence operations, it is sometimes hard to distinguish between the "noise" and the "signals." The nationalist extremists have not threatened violence to whites alone; they have held that club over the black community and have even used it against each other.* The returns are far from all in,

---

* From a Black Panther leader: "This means we have to out-talk the insanity that's propagated by the cultural nationalists, we have to out-organize them, even if it means returning to kicking their asses, knocking them in the head or physically eliminating them. We used to do these things, we used to whip them at parties, we used to jump on them in the streets, we used to jump on them in the movie shows, we used

and it would be well to wait another five years before making any judgment on what black Americans really want.

It cannot be stressed too strongly that, if the extreme nationalists have their way, the latent civil war between blacks and whites is also a latent civil war between blacks and blacks. The Black Panthers' demand for "community control of the police" could easily lead—and is, in fact, intended to lead—to Black Panthers' control of the black community. The totalitarian potential in the black nationalist movements threatens all democratic-minded blacks whose role in this struggle is peculiarly difficult and thankless. Whites who deal with the black nationalists as if they represent the entire black community reveal not only how little they know about the interplay of forces in that community, but how thoughtlessly they may be betraying those with whom they have most in common.

We may now restate the crucial question in another form: What are the limits of "integration" and "separatism" in a society is roughly 90 per cent white and 10 per cent black?

---

to fight them and we used to let them know that we were dissatisfied with their class positions" (Chief of Staff David Hilliard, "Enemies 'Within' Enemies 'Without,'" *The Black Panther*, September 6, 1969, p. 2).

One of Malcolm X's more dubious bequests was this stark version of the coming black civil war: "I read a little story once, and Mau Mau proved it. I read a story once where someone asked some group of people how many of them wanted freedom. They all put up their hand. Think there were about 300 of them. Then the person says, 'Well, how many of you are ready to kill anybody who gets in your way for freedom?' About fifty put up their hands. And he told those fifty, 'You stand over here.' That left 250 sitting who wanted freedom, but weren't ready to kill for it. So he told this fifty, 'Now you wanted freedom and you said you'd kill anybody who'd get in your way. You see those 250? You get them first. Some of them are your own brothers and sisters and mothers and fathers. But they're the ones who stand in the way of your freedom. They're afraid to do whatever is necessary to get it and they'll stop you from doing it.' I go for that. That's what the Mau Mau learned." (George Breitman, ed., *Malcolm X Speaks* [New York: Grove Press, 1965], p. 134.) Those who belong to the 250 cannot say they were not forewarned.

To explore these limits may well be the greatest contribution the Black Studies programs in our universities could make. They have the problem anyway, but they can undertake it as an onerous or as an ennobling ordeal and challenge. If the problem cannot be reflected on and experimented with in the universities, where else? We seem to be groping toward a new type of academic as well as political community—or, perhaps better, new community relationships. In both the academic and political spheres, there is bound to come the recognition that a new community is one thing, a new nation another—and those who seek a new community in order to incubate a new nation may well get neither.

That black nationalism may not be the answer is no recommendation for the old order. That the vast majority of black Americans cannot solve their problems by emigrating to another country or by setting up an independent state in this country does not mean that the only alternative is resignation to a permanently unequal status. It means that their struggle for freedom and equality must be fought out in the United States. It means, too, that the nature of the struggle must be understood for the long pull. Otherwise, there are bound to be more wasteful, spasmodic shifts of direction from "integration" to "separation" and back again. It is as much in the interest of whites as of blacks to understand the nature of this struggle because what is at stake is not a black nation or a white nation but an American nation. After two centuries, the American nation has not yet made full and equal citizens of at least one-tenth of its people, and as long as such inequality persists, this nation cannot claim to have reached full maturity. The enemies of peaceful change are so numerous and powerful that we are still in the phase in which the best policy is the one that moves forward on the broadest possible front.

What the change is finally going to be can be only dimly perceived at present. But of one thing we may be sure. As long as America permits black enclaves and ghettos, it cannot deny them representation of their own choosing—and remain true to itself or even avoid a conflagration. The democratic process itself must bring about far-reaching change in the relations of blacks and whites. Only political double bookkeeping and the most outrageous inequities have prevented such change earlier. The critical problem at this stage is whether the new political communities, whatever they may be, will relate more or less realistically to the other communities in the country or whether they will be infected with the nationalist fantasy and encourage a destructive—and self-destructive—separatism from the other communities. Once the fantasy sets in, no arrangement, however well-meaning, is workable. Whatever the road ahead, it can scarcely fail to be a hard one, full of bumps and sharp turns, threatening to many existing vested interests. If the democratic road is blocked, the nationalist fantasy will loom larger and larger, and the larger a fantasy becomes, the farther away it is from reality.

We still need some vision of a better future. If history can teach us nothing, we have nothing that can teach us. Historically, there has been a white fantasy to get rid of blacks, and a black fantasy to get rid of whites. After more than two centuries, it is high time for both whites and blacks to get rid of their fantasies instead of each other. Once that sinks in, we may begin to look forward to something better.

Reference Notes

Index

Reference Notes

1 / Colonization

1. The idea of returning blacks to Africa has apparently been traced back to 1714. Those who wish to know more of these proposals may consult Henry Noble Sherwood, "Early Negro Deportation Projects," *Mississippi Valley Historical Review*, March 1916, pp. 484–508. More recently, Professor Winthrop D. Jordan has gone over the same ground, including a detailed survey of Jefferson's views, in *White Over Black: American Attitudes Towards the Negro, 1550–1812* (Chapel Hill, N. C.: University of North Carolina Press, 1968), pp. 428–81 (Jefferson); pp. 542–82 (emancipation and colonization). Staughton Lynd's mordant essay "Slavery and the Founding Fathers" is vastly illuminating; reprinted in Melvin Drimmer, ed., *Black History* (New York: Doubleday, 1968), pp. 117–31—an excellent collection. Two other books may be useful in this respect: Matthew T. Mellon, *Early American Views on Negro Slavery*, with an Introduction by Richard B. Morris (1934, reprinted by Bergman Publishers, New York, 1969); and Robert McColley, *Slavery and Jeffersonian Virginia* (Urbana: University of Illinois Press, 1964, especially Ch. VI).

2. Roy P. Basler, ed., *The Collected Works of Abraham Lincoln* (New Brunswick, N.J.: Rutgers University Press, 1953), II, 245, 255–56, 409; V, 370–75. The August 1862 meeting is dealt with in Benjamin Quarles, *Lincoln and the Negro* (New York: Oxford University Press, 1962), pp. 115–17. In Lincoln's day, the two main colonization projects were located in Haiti and in Chiriqui, then the northernmost province of Panama. A good survey of white opinion in the period may be found in Robert H. Zoellner, "Negro Colonization: The Climate of Opinion Surrounding Lincoln, 1860–65," *Mid-America*, July 1960, pp. 131–50.

3. Cited by W. E. Burghardt Du Bois, *Black Reconstruction* (New York: Harcourt, 1935; reprinted by Russell & Russell), p. 149.

4. Philip S. Foner, ed., *The Life and Writings of Frederick Douglass* (New York: International Publishers, 1955), IV, 316 (April 14, 1876).

5. Philip J. Staudenraus, *The African Colonization Movement 1816–1865* (New York: Columbia University Press, 1961), p. 249.

6. According to one study, opposition to colonizationism was much stronger in the North than in the South (Louis R. Mehlinger, "The Attitude of the Free Negro Toward African Colonization," *The Journal of Negro History*, July 1916, pp. 276–301).

7. Bella Gross, *"Freedom's Journal* and the Rights of All," *The Journal of Negro History*, July 1932, pp. 262–68, 279.

8. Herbert Aptheker, ed., *A Documentary History of the Negro People in the United States* (New York: Citadel Press, 1951), I, 109. This collection contains indispensable source material.

9. Charles H. Wesley, *Richard Allen, Apostle of Freedom* (Washington, D.C.: The Associated Publishers, 1935), p. 50. The Methodists were most successful in converting Negroes, who, by 1796, constituted one-fifth of the total membership. But with more Negro Methodists came more segregated "Negro Pews" and other forms of discrimination, which brought about a Negro rebellion against these practices. In a famous incident in November 1787 in Philadelphia, a small group of Negroes, headed by Absalom Jones and Richard Allen, walked out of a Methodist church in protest against efforts made by a white trustee to force Jones to sit in the rear of the gallery (pp. 52–53).

10. William H. Pease and Jane H. Pease, *Black Utopia* (Madison, Wis.: The State Historical Society of Wisconsin, 1963), p. 160.

2 / Emigration

1. Benjamin Quarles, *The Negro in the Making of America* (New York: Macmillan, 1964), p. 96.
2. Wesley, *op. cit.,* pp. 66–67, 220.
3. Christopher Fyfe, *A History of Sierra Leone* (New York: Oxford University Press, 1962), pp. 14–19; Henry Noble Sherwood, "Early Negro Deportation Projects," *Mississippi Valley Historical Review,* March 1916, p. 501.
4. Sherwood, *ibid.,* p. 503.
5. Fyfe, *op. cit.,* p. 112. Sherwood says Hopkins was told that "Sierra Leone would receive twelve American families of good habits and discipline" (*op. cit.,* p. 506).
6. Paul Leicester Ford, ed., *The Works of Thomas Jefferson* (New York: Putnam's, 1905), IX, 374–75, 384–86; Fyfe, *op. cit.,* p. 112.
7. Henry Noble Sherwood, "Paul Cuffe," *The Journal of Negro History,* April 1923, pp. 153–229. Some interesting documents on Cuffe may be found in *Apropos of Africa,* compiled and edited by Adelaide Cromwell Hill and Martin Kilson (London: Frank Cass & Co., Ltd., 1969), pp. 11–20.
8. Staudenraus, *op. cit.,* p. 10.
9. *Ibid.,* p. 32.
10. William Loren Katz, *Eyewitness: The Negro in American History* (New York: Pitman, 1967), pp. 146–47.
11. William Lloyd Garrison, *Thoughts on African Colonization* (Boston: Garrison & Knapp, 1832), Part II, pp. 9–13.
12. Staudenraus, *op. cit.,* pp. 188–89.
13. Fyfe, *op. cit.,* p. 123.
14. Howard Bell, *A Survey of the Negro Convention Movement, 1830–1861,* unpublished Ph.D. dissertation, Northwestern University, 1953, pp. 12–33.
15. St. Clair Drake, "Negro Americans and the African Interest," in John P. Davis, ed., *American Negro Reference Book* (Englewood Cliffs, N.J.: Prentice-Hall, 1966), pp. 662–63.
16. Frank A. Rollin, *Life and Public Services of Martin R. Delany* (Boston: Lee & Shepard, 1868), pp. 19 and 22.
17. William Wells Brown, *The Black Man: His Antecedents, His Genius and His Achievements* (Boston: James Redpath, 1863), p. 175.
18. Bell, *op. cit.,* p. 134.
19. Lerone Bennett, Jr., *Before the Mayflower* (Penguin Books, rev. ed., 1966), p. 137; Howard H. Bell, Introduction to M. R. Delany and Robert Campbell, *Search for a Place* (Ann Arbor: University of Michigan Press, 1969), p. 8.

20. Carter G. Woodson, ed., *The Mind of the Negro As Reflected In Letters Written During The Crisis 1800–1860* (Washington D.C.: The Association for the Study of Negro Life and History, Inc., 1926), p. 293.

21. Martin R. Delany, *The Condition, Elevation, Emigration and Destiny of the Colored People of the United States* (Philadelphia: published by the author, 1852), pp. 48–49, 160, 171, 179, 193, 203.

22. Benjamin Quarles, Introduction to reprint of Delany, *op. cit.* (New York: Arno Press and *The New York Times*, 1968), p. 2.

23. Benjamin Brawley, *Negro Builders and Heroes* (Chapel Hill, N.C.: The University of North Carolina Press, 1937), p. 93.

24. M. R. Delany, *Official Report of the Niger Valley Exploring Party* (New York: Thomas Hamilton, 1861), p. 5. This work has been reprinted in Delany and Campbell, *op. cit.*, pp. 23–148.

25. As a result of the Fugitive Slave Act of 1850, the flight of Negroes increased greatly in the next decade, most of it to Canada. It was estimated that from 15,000 to 20,000 Negroes entered Canada from 1850 to 1860, increasing the Negro population there from about 40,000 to nearly 60,000 (Fred Landon, "The Negro Migration to Canada after the Passing of the Fugitive Slave Act," *The Journal of Negro History*, January 1920, p. 22). The story of the main organizer of this movement was told by Fred Landon, "Henry Bibb, a Colonizer," *ibid.*, October 1920, pp. 437–47.

26. *Proceedings of the National Emigration Convention*, Cleveland, Ohio, August 24–26, 1854 (Pittsburgh, Pa., 1854), pp. 38, 65 (Canada), 69 (recommendation on emigration), 21 (resolution), 73 (foreign mission), 25–26 (platform).

     The platform contained the following planks: No. 12: "That, as men and equals, we demand every political right, privilege and position to which whites are eligible in the United States, and we will either attain to these, or accept of nothing." No. 18: "That, as a people, we will never be satisfied nor contented until we occupy a position where we are acknowledged a necessary *constituent* in the *ruling element* of the country in which we live" (italics in original).

     The Reverend J. T. Holly later claimed that the convention had divided into "three parties," one represented by Delany, who wanted to go to the Niger Valley in Africa, another by James M. Whitfield of Buffalo, New York, who preferred Central America, and a third by Holly, who supported Haiti. Holly also said that "all these parties were recognized and embraced by the Convention. Dr. Delany was given a commission to go to Africa in the Niger Valley, Whitfield to go to Central America and Holly to Hayti [sic], to enter into negotiations with the authorities of these various countries for Negro emigrants and to report to future conventions." See John W. Cromwell, *The Negro in American History* (Washington: The American Negro Academy, 1914), pp. 43–44. There is no evidence in the *Proceedings* that such commissions were given in 1854.

27. Delany, *Official Report of the Niger Valley Exploring Party, op. cit.,* pp. 8–9.

28. *Ibid.,* p. 10.

29. *Ibid.,* p. 12.

30. Bell, *A Survey of the Negro Convention Movement, op. cit.,* p. 244.

31. Delany's novel appeared in *The Anglo-African Magazine* in the issues dated January to July 1859.

32. The account in *The Times* (London) appeared in *The Evening Post* (New York), July 31, 1860, p. 3. Other accounts vary slightly. According to Judge Longstreet, Lord Brougham was somewhat more provocative: "I call the attention of Mr. Dallas to the fact that there is a negro present (or among the delegates), and I hope he will have no scruples on that account." Rollin, *op. cit.,* pp. 104–105. Delany had still another shorter version: "I would remind my friend, Mr. Dallas, that there is a negro member of the Congress" (*ibid.,* p. 118). Delany gave his own reply as follows: "I rise, your Royal Highness, to thank his lordship, the unflinching friend of the negro, for the remarks he has made in reference to myself, and to assure your Royal Highness and his lordship that *I am a man*" (*ibid.,* p. 119).

33. *Diary of George Mifflin Dallas* (Philadelphia: J. B. Lippincott, 1892), pp. 407–408. Oddly, Delany himself believed that Dallas had not been so disturbed by Lord Brougham's action: "Mr. Dallas, seeming to receive this kindly, bowed and smiled" (Rollin, *op. cit.,* p. 118).

34. John Donald Wade, *Augustus Baldwin Longstreet* (New York: Macmillan, 1924), pp. 325–27.

35. Rollin, *op. cit.,* p. 106.

36. *Ibid.,* p. 121.

37. *The Evening Post,* July 31, 1860; *The New York Tribune,* August 1, 1860; *The World,* August 3, 1860; *The New York Times,* August 1, 1860; *The New York Herald,* August 2, 1860.

38. Leon F. Litwack, *North of Slavery* (Chicago: The University of Chicago Press, 1961), p. 262.

39. Rollin, *op. cit.*, p. 141.

40. Benjamin Quarles, *Lincoln and the Negro* (New York: Oxford University Press, 1962) p. 160.

41. Rollin, *op. cit.*, pp. 166–71. As far as I can make out, this meeting between Lincoln and Delany is not mentioned in any biography of Lincoln. The Basler edition of Lincoln's collected works contains the one-sentence card written by Lincoln to Stanton about Delany, citing Rollin as the source, but gives nothing of the conversation between Lincoln and Delany (Roy P. Basler, ed., *The Collected Works of Abraham Lincoln* [New Brunswick: Rutgers University Press, 1953], VIII, 272–73). Quarles also mentions the card (*ibid.*, p. 205) but not the conversation. Rollin took pains to note that his version of the Lincoln-Delany interview was given in "Major Delany's own language" (p. 166). The failure of all of Lincoln's biographers to mention Delany or this incident, a most colorful and significant one, is hard to explain.

42. Dudley Taylor Cornish, *The Sable Arm* (New York: Longmans, Green, 1956), pp. 216–17. Delany was only "nominally assigned" to the 104th, but was actually detailed to special duty with the military governor, Brigadier-General Rufus B. Saxton. See Joel Williamson, *After Slavery* (Chapel Hill, N.C.: University of North Carolina Press, 1965), p. 28.

43. Rollin, *op. cit.*, 2d ed. (1883), p. 279.

44. Francis Butler Simkins and Robert Hilliard Woody, *South Carolina During Reconstruction* (Chapel Hill, N.C.: University of North Carolina Press, 1932), p. 55.

45. Wade, *op. cit.*, pp. 329–30. This writer, then of the University of Georgia, permitted himself the liberty of calling Delany "an objectionable and absurd mountebank" (p. 329).

46. Simkins and Woody, *op. cit.*, p. 472 *n*.

47. David Duncan Wallace, *South Carolina, A Short History* (Chapel Hill, N.C.: University of North Carolina Press, 1951), p. 592. Another Southern historian wrote of Delany: "Major Delany was a genuine negro. . . . After the war he was connected with the Freedmen's Bureau on the South Carolina coast, and in that relation had made a good impression on the white people. . . . He was a man of unusual intelligence and a very good speaker" (John S. Reynolds, *Reconstruction in South Carolina, 1865–1877* [Columbia, S.C.: The State Co., 1905], p. 279).

48. Simkins and Woody, *op. cit.,* p. 473 *n.*
49. Wallace, *op. cit.,* p. 602.
50. Hampton M. Jarrell, *Wade Hampton and the Negro* (Columbia, S.C.: University of South Carolina Press, 1949), p. 58; Ernest McPherson Lander, Jr., *A History of South Carolina, 1865–1960* (Chapel Hill, N.C.: University of North Carolina Press, 1960), p. 19.
51. Simkins and Woody, *op. cit.,* pp. 499–500.
52. Alfred B. Williams, *Hampton and His Red Shirts* (Charleston, S.C.: Walker, Evans & Cogswell, 1935), p. 261.
53. Reynolds, *op. cit.,* pp. 378–80; Williams, *op. cit.,* pp. 270–74; Jarrell, *op. cit.,* p. 69.
54. Jarrell, *op cit.,* p. 99.
55. Williamson, *op. cit.,* pp. 279, 357, 358–59. For some reason not clear to me, Williamson characterizes Delany as "an egomaniac and insufferable pedant" (p. 28).
56. Elsie M. Lewis, "The Political Mind of the Negro, 1865–1900," in Charles E. Wynes, ed., *The Negro in the South Since 1865* (University, Ala.: University of Alabama Press, 1965), p. 32.
57. Alrutheus Ambush Taylor, *The Negro in South Carolina During the Reconstruction* (Washington, D.C.: The Association for the Study of Negro Life and History, 1924), pp. 209–210. J. J. Wright was an Associate Justice of the State Supreme Court. In 1877 Delany testified against the corrupt practices of a successful white candidate for United States Senator (p. 277).
58. *Ibid.,* p. 211.
59. Simkins and Woody, *op. cit.,* p. 511.
60. Williams, *op. cit.,* p. 222.
61. Jarrell, *op. cit.,* p. 41.
62. Sir George Campbell, *Black and White: The Outcome of a Visit to the United States* (London: Chatto and Windus, 1879), p. 341.
63. George Brown Tindall, *South Carolina Negroes 1877–1900* (Columbia, S.C.: University of South Carolina Press, 1952), pp. 156, 160–61, 165, 289.
64. Campbell, *op. cit.,* p. 347.
65. Rollin, *op. cit.,* p. 77.
66. Tindall, *op. cit.,* p. 38.
67. Martin R. Delany, *Principia of Ethnology: The Origin of Races and Color, with an Archaeological Compendium of Ethiopian and Egyptian Civilization* (Philadelphia: Harper & Bros., 1879), pp. 105–109. There was a second edition in 1880.

68. Henry Highland Garnet, *The Past and the Present Condition, and the Destiny of the Colored Race,* reprinted in Howard Brotz, ed., *Negro Social and Political Thought 1850–1920* (New York: Basic Books, 1966), pp. 199–202.
69. *Ibid.,* pp. 191–94.
70. William Brewer, "Henry Highland Garnet," *The Journal of Negro History,* January 1928, p. 51.
71. J. Theodore Holly, "Thoughts on Hayti," *The Anglo-African Magazine,* August 1858, pp. 241–42.
72. Edwin S. Redkey, *Black Exodus* (New Haven: Yale University Press, 1969), p. 37.
73. Aptheker, ed., *op. cit.,* II, 757.
74. *Ibid.,* II, 646–48.
75. Foner, ed., *op. cit.,* IV, 513.
76. Redkey, *op. cit.,* pp. 59–70.
77. *Ibid.,* pp. 195–242.
78. Alfred W. Reynolds, "The Alabama Negro Colony in Mexico; 1894–96," *The Alabama Review,* October 1952, pp. 243–68, and January 1953, pp. 31–58.
79. Redkey, *op. cit.,* pp. 291, 297, 299–301.
80. Holly, *op. cit.,* November 1859, pp. 364–66.
81. Redkey, *op. cit.,* p. 35.
82. Howard Brotz has edited an excellent anthology of Delany, Blyden, Garnet, as well as Douglass, Washington, Du Bois, Garvey, and others: *Negro Social and Political Thought 1850–1920, op. cit.* For their influence on African nationalism, see George Shepperson, "Notes on Negro American Influences on the Emergence of African Nationalism," *Journal of African History,* Vol. I, No. 2 (1960), pp. 299–312 (reprinted in *Black History,* pp. 493–512). Blyden, Delany, and others are also treated in an essay by Hollis R. Lynch, "Pan-Negro Nationalism in the New World, Before 1862," reprinted in another excellent collection: August Meier and Elliott Rudwick, eds., *The Making of Black America* (New York: Atheneum, 1969), I, 42–65.

Two other pioneer essays which deal with colonization and emigration may be noted: Herbert Aptheker, "Consciousness of Negro Nationality to 1900," *Political Affairs,* June 1949, reprinted in *Toward Negro Freedom* (New York: New Century Publishers, 1956, pp. 104–111); and August Meier, "The Emergence of Negro Nationalism," *The Midwest Journal,* Winter 1951–52, pp. 96–104, and Summer 1952, pp. 95–111.

3 / From Pan-Africa to Back-to-Africa

1. William Edward Burghardt Du Bois, "The Conservation of Races," in Howard Brotz, ed., *op. cit.*, pp. 483–92.
2. W. E. B. Du Bois, *Dusk of Dawn* (New York: Harcourt, Brace, 1940; Schocken Books, 1968), pp. 197–200, 306.
3. At no time during his lifetime did Du Bois accept the old Communist doctrine of "self-determination." He once set the record straight by writing: "When we compare American Negroes with other groups, we are not comparing nations, nor even cultural groups; since American Negroes do not form a nation and are not likely to if their present fight for political integration succeeds" (*Freedom*, January 1953, p. 7). The final proviso may have left the door open, and it is anyone's guess how Du Bois might have reacted to the separatist movement of the late 1960s.
4. Rayford Logan, ed., *What the Negro Wants* (Chapel Hill, N.C.: University of North Carolina Press, 1944), p. 60.
5. Du Bois, *Dusk of Dawn, op. cit.*, p. 303.
6. *Philosophy and Opinions of Marcus Garvey,* compiled by Amy Jacques Garvey (London: Frank Cass, 1967, 2 vols. in one), II, 238.
7. Edmund David Cronon, *Black Moses* (Madison, Wis.: University of Wisconsin Press, 1955), p. 190 (cited from *The Crisis,* XXVIII, 8–9).
8. *Philosophy and Opinions of Marcus Garvey, op. cit.*, I, 5; II, 23, 34.
9. *Ibid.*, I, 29.
10. *Ibid.*, II, 71.
11. *Ibid.*, II, 38, 126.
12. *Ibid.*, II, 46.
13. The standard biography of Garvey is Cronon's *Black Moses.*
14. Gunnar Myrdal, with the assistance of Richard Sterner and Arnold Rose, *An American Dilemma* (New York: Harper & Bros., 1944), p. 749.
15. John Hope Franklin, *From Slavery to Freedom* (New York: Alfred A. Knopf, 1952), p. 483.
16. Harold Cruse, *The Crisis of the Negro Intellectual* (New York: Morrow, 1967), p. 82.

4 / Self-Determination

1. Paul Leicester Ford, ed., *op. cit.*, IX, 315–19.
2. Carter G. Woodson, *A Century of Negro Migration* (Wash-

ington, D.C.: The Association for the Study of Negro Life and History, 1918), pp. 10–11.

3. Aptheker, ed., *op. cit.*, I, 70–71.

4. Woodson, *op. cit.*, p. 66.

5. William Lloyd Garrison, *op. cit.*, Part II, p. 46 (Trenton), p. 49 (Lewiston).

6. In *American Communism and Soviet Russia* (New York: Viking Press, 1960), pp. 322–26, I have reconstructed the story of Cyril V. Briggs and the African Blood Brotherhood.

7. Cronon, *op. cit.*, p. 75.

8. Draper, *op. cit.*, pp. 332–35.

9. *Philosophy and Opinions of Marcus Garvey, op. cit.*, II, 70, 72.

10. James S. Allen, *The Negro Question in the United States* (New York: International Publishers, 1936), pp. 14–17. The map appears on p. 17. Allen was unlucky in the publication of this book; it appeared just about the time the Communist Party was beginning to disentangle itself from the theory which it espoused.

11. I am now working on the third volume of my history of American Communism, dealing with the 1930s, in which this part of the story will be told in detail. The background is fully covered in the second volume, *American Communism and Soviet Russia*, Chapter 15.

12. "Resolution of the Communist International, October 1930," *The Communist Position on the Negro Question* (New York: Workers Library Publishers, 1931), p. 50.

13. George Breitman, ed., *Leon Trotsky on Black Nationalism and Self-Determination* (New York: Merit Publishers, 1967), pp. 13, 18, and 29. The latest Trotskyist program still gives Afro-Americans the option of deciding "to exercise their right of self-determination through the creation of a separate black nation or within the context of the creation of a single socialist republic along with insurgent white workers and other anti-capitalist forces" ("A Transitional Program for Black Liberation," resolution adopted at 23rd National Convention of Socialist Workers Party, Labor Day weekend, 1969, *International Socialist Review,* November–December 1969, pp. 67–68).

14. *Political Affairs,* November 1968, pp. 1–11 (Lightfoot); and March 1969 (James E. Jackson and Ted Bassett).

5 / The Nation of Islam

1. Most of what is known about Noble Drew Ali comes from Arthur H. Fauset, *Black Gods of the Metropolis* (Philadelphia: University of Pennsylvania Press, 1944), pp. 32–52; and Arna Bontemps and Jack Conroy, *They Seek a City* (New York: Doubleday, Doran, 1945), pp. 174–77—a revised edition of which is *Anyplace But Here* (New York: Hill and Wang, 1966), especially pp. 205–208.

2. Fauset, *op. cit.*, pp. 32–35.

3. Howard Brotz, *The Black Jews of Harlem* (New York: Free Press, 1964).

4. Erdmann Doane Beynon, "The Voodoo Cult Among Negro Migrants in Detroit," *The American Journal of Sociology*, May 1938, pp. 894–907. Fard's cult was then associated with "Voodoo" because of its alleged encouragement of human sacrifices. The foregoing account has been taken from Beynon's pioneer study. There is some further information in Bontemps and Conroy, *op. cit.*, pp. 178–82 (or *Anyplace But Here*, pp. 216–23), but this is largely based on Beynon.

5. C. Eric Lincoln, *The Black Muslims in America* (Boston: Beacon Press, 1961), p. 13.

6. This information comes from Elijah Muhammad, *Message To The Blackman in America* (Chicago: Muhammad Mosque No. 2, 1965), pp. 24–25. Elijah Muhammad says that Fard sent for him whenever he was arrested. Beynon (*op. cit.*, p. 896) says that Fard lived in Detroit from July 4, 1930, to June 30, 1934. Bontemps and Conroy (*op. cit.*, p. 182) say that Fard left Detroit and disappeared in 1933. The best authority would undoubtedly be Elijah Muhammad.

7. Daniel Burley, Foreword to *Message To The Blackman in America*, p. xiii. The rest of this paragraph is based on Elijah Muhammad, *op. cit.*, pp. 178–79.

8. The story of Yakub and the rest of this cosmology have been taken, almost verbatim, from Elijah Muhammad, *op. cit.*, where they are scattered throughout the book, but appear especially on pp. 110–22. I have tried to organize the various fragments of the story into a continuous whole.

9. *Ibid.*, pp. 169, 218, 223.

10. *Ibid.*, pp. 234, 275, 161, 317.

11. Speech at Washington, D.C., May 31, 1959, cited by E. U. Essien-Udom, *Black Nationalism* (Chicago: University of Chicago Press, 1962), p. 286.

12. *New York Times,* November 23 and December 12, 1969; *Wall Street Journal,* November 25, 1969.
13. Elijah Muhammad, *op. cit.,* p. 48.
14. *Ibid.,* p. 162.
15. *Ibid.,* p. 174.
16. *Ibid.,* p. 183.
17. *Ibid.,* p. 163.
18. Essien-Udom, *op. cit.,* p. 167.

6 / Malcolm X

1. *The Autobiography of Malcolm X,* with the assistance of Alex Haley (New York: Grove Press, 1965).
2. George Breitman, ed., *Malcolm X Speaks* (New York: Grove Press, 1965), p. 5. This book contains a selection of Malcolm X's speeches and statements in his last year.
3. *The Autobiography of Malcolm X, op. cit.,* p. 333. The change may have started earlier. In a speech in Cleveland on April 3, 1964, ten days before his departure, he protested that what he said "doesn't mean that we're anti-white, but it does mean we're anti-exploitation, we're anti-degradation, we're anti-oppression" (*Malcolm X Speaks,* pp. 24–25).
4. *The Autobiography of Malcolm X,* p. 366 (italics in original).
5. *Malcolm X Speaks,* p. 112.
6. *Ibid.,* p. 144.
7. *The Autobiography of Malcolm X,* p. 367 (italics in original).
8. *Malcolm X Speaks,* pp. 7–10.
9. George Breitman, *The Last Year of Malcolm X* (New York: Schocken Books, 1967), p. 57 (italics in original).
10. *Malcolm X Speaks,* p. 20.
11. *Ibid.,* p. 36.
12. *Ibid.,* p. 129 (December 20, 1964).
13. *The Autobiography of Malcolm X,* pp. 333–34.
14. *Malcolm X Speaks,* p. 212. There is also a predominantly pro-black Nationalist version in William H. Friedland and Harry Edwards, "Confrontation at Cornell," *The Transformation of Activism,* ed. by August Meier (*Trans-*Action Books, 1970, pp. 68–89).
15. *Ibid.,* pp. 62–63, 210.
16. *Ibid.,* p. 38.
17. *The Autobiography of Malcolm X,* pp. 367–68, 375 (italics in original).
18. The full texts may be found in Breitman, *op. cit.,* pp. 105–24.
19. *Malcolm X Speaks,* pp. 197, 212–13.

20. *Ibid.*, pp. 38, 203.
21. Breitman, *op. cit.*, p. 68.
22. *The Autobiography of Malcolm X*, p. 339 (italics in original).

7 / The Black Panthers

1. This version of the origins comes mainly from Gene Marine, *The Black Panthers* (New York: New American Library, 1969), pp. 12–16, 24–34. I have followed it for biographical details, not otherwise available. But one of Huey's older brothers, Lee Edward Newton, has said that Huey was born in California, not in Louisiana (interview, *The Black Panther*, May 19, 1969, p. 20). Seale told of his army career in *The Black Panther*, September 13, 1969, p. 17. Marine's book is mainly devoted to the Panthers' fights with the police and courts, and tells little about their program and make-up. Seale told how they wrote the Platform and Program in *The Black Panther*, October 18, 1969, p. 2.

2. Twenty-nine chapters and branches were listed in *The Black Panther*, November 1, 1969, p. 20. Seale had previously claimed thirty-nine chapters (*ibid.*, October 25, 1969, p. 10). One reporter stated that the Panthers had claimed to have set up thirty-five chapters which had had a membership of about five thousand at its peak but had been cut to about half by the end of 1969 (Earl Caldwell, *The New York Times*, December 14, 1969). A government estimate was said to be as low as twelve hundred (*Life*, February 6, 1970, p. 18).

3. The Platform and Program, *What We Want What We Believe*, appears in every issue of *The Black Panther*.

4. *Essays From the Minister of Defense Huey Newton* (1968), pp. 3, 5, 11.

5. Frantz Fanon, *The Wretched of the Earth* (New York: Grove Press, 1963), pp. 108, 120, etc.

6. *The Black Panther*, March 16, 1968, p. 16. See also Huey Newton, "The Black Panthers," *Ebony*, August 1969, p. 110, in which he said: "The Black Panthers are revolutionary nationalists. We do not believe that it is necessary to go back to the culture of eleventh century Africa. In reality, we must deal with the dynamic present in order to forge a progressive future. We feel no need to retreat to the past, although we respect our African heritage. The things that are useful in the African heritage we will use to deal with the forces that are working on us today. Those things that are outdated, that are antique, we will look upon with respect, and a fact of our heritage, but

not as the basis for a pattern of behavior to follow in the present time."

7. *The Black Panther,* March 3, 1969, p. 4. Murray was the English instructor at San Francisco State College whose dismissal, for having allegedly told students to bring guns on campus, set off months of disorder there. Murray denied the charge, but he made a speech at Fresno State College, published in *The Black Panther* of November 16, 1968, in which he advised that "if you want campus autonomy, if the students want to run the college, if the cracker administrators don't go for it, then you control it with the gun." Murray was replaced by Ray "Masai" Hewitt as Minister of Education in 1969 apparently because Murray experienced a renewal of religious faith and dropped out of the movement (*The New York Times,* October 20, 1969).

8. "The Roots of the Party," *The Black Panther,* May 25, 1969, p. 4.

9. *The Black Panther,* May 31, 1969, p. 16. By the end of 1969, chief of staff David Hilliard went even further: "The Black Panther Party is not going to support any B.S.U. [Black Student Union] policy that asks for an autonomous program that excludes other individuals" (*ibid.,* December 27, 1969, p. 3).

10. "Huey Newton Talks to the Movement" (interview originally published in *The Movement* [San Francisco], August 1968, reprinted by Students for a Democratic Society, 1968, p. 4).

11. "The Roots of the Party," *loc. cit.*

12. Newton, "The Black Panthers," *Ebony, loc. cit.,* pp. 107–108.

13. *Liberator,* September 1969, p. 5. Another report of the same conference stated that at least 85 per cent and perhaps 90 per cent of the crowd was white, almost all of them students (Robert A. Jones, *The Nation,* August 11, 1969, p. 102).

14. *The Black Panther,* August 30, 1969, p. 13.

15. *Ibid.,* August 2, 1969, p. 4.

16. *Essays From the Minister of Defense Huey Newton,* pp. 19–20.

17. *The New York Times,* July 4, 1969.

18. *Ramparts,* September 1969, p. 31.

19. *The Black Panther,* October 18, 1969, p. 9.

20. Daniel H. Watts, *Liberator,* September 1969, p. 3.

21. *The Black Panther,* March 16, 1968, p. 8.

22. "Quotations from Huey," *The Black Panther,* February 17, 1969, p. 4.

23. *Ibid.,* August 2, 1969, p. 17.

24. *Ibid.,* August 9, 1969, p. 13.

25. Newton, "The Black Panthers," *Ebony, loc. cit.,* p. 110.

26. *The Black Panther,* September 27, 1969, pp. 10–11.

27. *Ibid.,* December 6, 1969, pp. 10–11. This statement was made September 13, 1969.

28. Robert Scheer, ed., *Eldridge Cleaver: Post-Prison Writings and Speeches* (New York: Random House, 1969), pp. 57–72. This article originally appeared in *Ramparts,* April–May 1968.

29. *Ibid.,* p. 187.

8 / Black Power

1. Jack Newfield, "Question of SNCC," *The Nation,* July 19, 1965, pp. 38–40. The first three years of SNCC are treated in Howard Zinn, *SNCC, The New Abolitionists* (Boston: Beacon Press, 1964).

2. Stokely Carmichael, speech delivered in Chicago, July 22, 1966, reprinted in Gilbert Osofsky, ed., *The Burden of Race* (New York: Harper & Row, 1967), pp. 629–36.

3. Stokely Carmichael, "What We Want," *The New York Review of Books,* September 22, 1966, p. 5.

4. *Ibid.,* p. 6.

5. Stokely Carmichael and Charles V. Hamilton, *Black Power* (New York: Vintage Books, 1967), p. 6.

6. *Ibid.,* pp. 44, 46, 47, 84.

7. Stokely Carmichael, "Black Power," in *The Dialectics of Liberation,* edited by David Cooper (London: Penguin Books, 1968), pp. 150–74.

8. Interview with Jonathan Power, *The Sunday Times Magazine* (London), November 2, 1969, p. 28.

9. Stokely Carmichael, "Pan-Africanism—Land and Power," *The Black Scholar* (San Francisco), November 1969, pp. 36–43.

10. Olly Leeds, *Liberator,* February 1969, p. 7.

11. Julius Lester, *Look Out Whitey! Black Power's Gon' Get Your Mama!* (New York: Grove Press, paperback edition, 1969), pp. 138–40.

12. *Ibid.,* pp. 87–89.

13. LeRoi Jones, *Home* (New York: Morrow, 1966), pp. 105–115.

14. Harold Cruse, *op. cit.,* p. 458.

15. *Ibid.,* pp. 433, 448.

16. *Ibid.,* p. 557.

17. *Ibid.,* p. 439.

18. *Ibid.,* pp. 554–55.

19. *Ibid.,* pp. 452, 169.

20. *Ibid.,* pp. 364, 483–84.

21. *Ibid.,* p. 455.

9 / The Land Question

1. John Henrik Clarke, "The New Afro-American Nationalism," *Freedomways,* Fall 1961, pp. 285–95.
2. E.U. Essien-Udom, "The Nationalist Movements in Harlem," in John Henrik Clarke, ed., *Harlem: A Community in Transition* (New York: Citadel Press, 1964), pp. 97–104.
3. Robert S. Browne, "The Case for Black Separatism," *Ramparts,* December 1967, p. 50.
4. LeRoi Jones, *op. cit.,* pp. 238–50.
5. LeRoi Jones, "The Need for a Cultural Base to Civil Rites & Bpower Mooments," in Floyd B. Barbour, ed., *The Black Power Revolt* (New York: Collier Books, 1969), pp. 136–44.
6. *Liberator,* June 1969, p. 10.
7. Thomas A. Johnson, *The New York Times,* August 24 and August 26, 1969.
8. Robert Sherrill, "We Want Georgia, South Carolina, Louisiana, Mississippi and Alabama—Right Now," *Esquire,* January 1969, pp. 72–75 and 146–48.
9. *Amsterdam News* (New York), March 22, 1969, p. 25.
10. *Ibid.,* April 19, 1969, p. 23.
11. Sherrill, *op. cit.,* p. 148.
12. Floyd McKissick, *Three-Fifths of a Man* (New York: Macmillan, 1969), pp. 145–46, 163–64.
13. Alex Poinsett, "Roy Innis: Nation-Builder," *Ebony,* October 1969, p. 176.
14. This entire subject is excellently presented in Reynolds Farley, "The Urbanization of Negroes in the United States," *Journal of Social History,* Spring 1968, pp. 241–58.
15. Philip M. Hauser, "Demographic Factors in the Integration of the Negro in the United States," *Daedalus,* Fall 1965, p. 852. This is another excellent treatment. *Daedalus* devoted two full issues to "The American Negro," Fall 1965 and Winter 1966, before the issue of black nationalism had become acute.
16. John Herbers, *The New York Times,* January 6, 1970.
17. Stokely Carmichael, *The Black Scholar, op. cit.,* p. 39.
18. *Ibid.,* p. 41.

10 / Black Studies

1. Robert S. Browne, "The Challenge of Black Student Organizations," *Freedomways,* Fall 1968, p. 331. John H. Bunzel, in "Black Studies at San Francisco State," *The Public Interest,*

Fall 1968, says that a Black Arts and Culture Series was instituted as part of the Experimental College in the fall semester of 1966 (p. 27). A somewhat later story may be found in Ralph M. Goldman, "Confrontation at S.F. State," *Dissent,* March–April 1969, pp. 167–79.

2. Bunzel, *op. cit.,* p. 23. Professor Bunzel was Chairman of the Political Science Department at San Francisco State College.

3. *The Black Panther,* January 25, 1969, p. 10.

4. *Ibid.,* March 16, 1969, p. 14.

5. Bunzel, *op. cit.,* pp. 28–29.

6. Roger A. Fischer, "Ghetto and Gown: The Birth of Black Studies," *Current History,* November 1969, pp. 292, 295.

7. *Ibid.,* p. 293.

8. Stephen Lythcott, "The Case for Black Studies," *The Antioch Review,* Summer 1969, pp. 149–54.

9. Kenneth B. Clark, "A Charade of Power: Black Students at White Colleges," *The Antioch Review,* Summer 1969, p. 147.

10. *Cornell Daily Sun,* December 9, 1968.

11. *Ibid.,* December 13, 1968.

12. *Ibid.,* December 18, 1968.

13. *Ibid.*

14. Allan P. Sindler, "A Case Study of a University's Pattern of Error," a paper presented at the annual meeting of the American Political Science Association, September 1969, New York City, p. 9. Professor Sindler was Chairman of the Department of Politics. Professor Sindler's paper was extremely critical of the Cornell administration. For an anti-Sindler point of view, see Douglas Dowd, "Cornell's Uptight Spring," *New Politics,* October 1969 (Vol. VII, No. 4), pp. 30–44.

15. *Campus Unrest at Cornell,* Report of Special Trustee Committee, submitted September 5, 1969 (The Office of University Publications, Cornell University, 1969), p. 53.

16. *Guns on Campus: Student Protest at Cornell* (Chicago: Urban Research Corp., 1970), p. 18. This report is mainly valuable for its recapitulation of the events of April 1969. It says that Jones's radio threat was aimed at three professors only; *Campus Unrest at Cornell, op. cit.,* says that he threatened President Perkins, four top administrators, and three professors (p. 24).

17. *Guns on Campus, op. cit.,* p. 18. Sindler, *op cit.,* p. 18, says that most of those threatened, including President Perkins, moved their families for the night.

18. From a transcript of the speech by Thomas W. Jones, June 29, 1969. Excerpts from this speech were published in the *Cornell*

Alumni News, September 1969, pp. 29–30, but these excerpts did not include all the passages I have quoted.

19. Clark, *op. cit.,* pp. 145–46.
20. *The Black Panther,* May 11, 1969, p. 5.
21. James Turner, "Black Students and Their Changing Perspective," *Ebony,* August 1969, pp. 135–40.
22. *Newsweek,* August 11, 1969, p. 38.
23. Dr. Vincent Harding, "Black Students and the 'Impossible' Revolution," *Ebony,* August 1969, pp. 141–46.
24. Carmichael, *The Black Scholar, op. cit.,* p. 43.
25. James Turner, "An Approach to Black Studies: Concept and Plan of the African Studies and Research Center," reprinted in *Cornell Chronicle,* published by the Office of Public Information, Cornell University, October 2, 1969, pp. 4–6.
26. This paragraph is based on: Armstead L. Robinson, "Appendix—Afro-American Studies Major At Yale," *Black Studies in the University* (New Haven: Yale University Press, 1969), pp. 225–31; W.H.J., "How Black Studies Happened," *Yale Alumni Magazine,* May 1969, pp. 22–27; "Yale University Afro-American Studies," *Bulletin of Yale University,* June 1, 1969, pp. 46–51 (reprint).
27. Sidney W. Mintz, "Afro-American Studies at Yale," 6 pp. (mimeographed).
28. Gerald A. McWorter, *Black Studies in the University, op. cit.,* pp. 72–73.
29. For those interested in the more general problem of black students at predominantly white universities, three other experiences may be useful: Richard J. Margolis, "The Two Nations at Wesleyan University," *The New York Times Magazine,* January 18, 1970, pp. 9, 49–64; B. Nelson, "Brandeis: How a Liberal Reacts to a Black Take-Over," *Science,* March 28, 1969, pp. 1431–34; Paul B. Abrahams, "Black Thursday at Oshkosh [Wisconsin State University]," *The Crisis,* November 1969, pp. 359–61, 373–81. *The Journal of Negro Education,* Fall 1969, pp. 423–52, contained six short informative and thoughtful studies of the problem.
30. Ray Rogers, "Black Guns on Campus," *The Nation,* May 5, 1969, pp. 558–60.
31. *The Black Panther,* September 6, 1969, p. 10.
32. Gene Marine, *op. cit.,* p. 209.
33. Eldridge Cleaver, "The Black Man's Stake in Vietnam," *The Black Panther,* March 23, 1969, p. 16.

11 / Limits

1. J. H. O'Dell, "A Special Variety of Colonialism," *Freedomways,* Winter 1967, pp. 7–9.

2. This theory was presented by W. Lloyd Warner and Allison Davis in Edgar Thompson, ed., *Race Relations and the Race Problem* (Durham, N.C.: Duke University Press, 1939), pp. 219–45. But the "caste" theory goes at least as far back as Charles H. Cooley (1897) and W. I. Thomas (1904). In fact, an outstanding Negro scholar, Dr. James McCune Smith, discussed slavery in terms of "caste" in *The Anglo-African Magazine,* January 1859, p. 16. For a brief survey of the sociological tradition on this question, see E. Franklin Frazier, *On Race Relations* (Chicago: University of Chicago Press, 1968), pp. 30–42.

3. Gunnar Myrdal, with the assistance of Richard Sterner and Arnold Rose, *An American Dilemma* (New York: Harper & Bros., 1944), p. 667.

4. Frazier, *op. cit.,* p. 46; Oliver Cromwell Cox, *Caste, Class and Race* (New York: Doubleday, 1948). Bruno Bettelheim has taken the extreme position that "what makes us uneasy in our relations with Negroes is exactly what makes us uneasy in our relations to the poor" (*The Nation,* October 19, 1963, p. 233).

5. Myrdal et al., *op cit.,* pp. li, 117.

6. I have followed the account by Carlton B. Goodlett in *Ramparts,* November 1967, pp. 99–101.

7. Maurice Zeitlin, *Ramparts,* November 1967, pp. 109–110.

8. Eldridge Cleaver, *ibid.,* p. 111.

9. W. H. Ferry, "Black Colonies: A Modest Proposal," *The Center Magazine* (Santa Barbara, Calif.), January 1968, pp. 74–76.

10. W. H. Ferry, "Farewell to Integration," *ibid.,* March 1968, pp. 35–40.

11. S. E. Anderson, "The Fragmented Movement," *Negro Digest,* Sept.–Oct. 1968, pp. 4–10.

12. Cited by Bayard Rustin, "The Failure of Black Separatism," *Harper's,* January 1970, p. 31.

13. See *Palo Alto Times,* August 18, 1969, p. 35, for a report on this development. The schools are privately run with funds partially donated by the Office of Economic Opportunity and a San Mateo County agency.

Index